Advance praise for

Create A Great Deal:
The Art of Real Estate Negotiating

From Real Estate Coaches and Instructors

"Tim Burrell has infused the real estate experience with negotiating knowledge, giving useful strategies to every piece in the process. His *Create A Great Deal* is a contribution to the industry and a gift for anyone desiring better results in their negotiating skills."

> — **Howard Brinton**, premier real estate coach, founder and CEO of STAR POWER Systems, Past National President of the Council of Residential Specialists. www.GoStarPower.com

"Tim Burrell's new book on negotiating, *Create a Great Deal*, is easy to read, filled with real world examples and full of smart, creative ideas that will take your negotiating skills to the next level. Read this book—your buyers and sellers will benefit and so will your bottom line. Who knew negotiating and reading about it could be such fun?!"

> — **Laurie Moore-Moore**, founder of The Institute for Luxury Home Marketing, co-founder and former co-editor of REAL Trends and creator of the Certified Luxury Home Marketing Specialist designation. She is the author of *Rich Buyer, Rich Seller*. www.LuxuryHomeMarketing.com

"In any market, but especially in today's market, REALTORS® need negotiating talent. Tim knows negotiating, and better yet, he knows how to get his no-fail information and strategies across to you. If you need to improve your negotiation skills, this is the book for you!"

> — **Allen F. Hainge**, CRS Instructor, premier real estate coach, Founder and President of the CyberStars®, he is the author of *Dominate!* and *Secrets of the CyberStars®.* www.CyberStars.net

"Tim Burrell's book, *Create a Great Deal*, is the most comprehensive real estate negotiation book ever written for the real estate industry. Even if you have been negotiating real estate deals for 30 years or more, Burrell's proven approaches will provide you with more new tools in your negotiating toolbox than you can possibly imagine. If you want to sky rocket your negotiation skills, *Create a Great Deal* is the one book you need today to make your business soar tomorrow."

— **Bernice Ross**, syndicated columnist, speaker and author. Inman News calls her "America's Top Real Estate Coach." She is the author of *Waging War on Real Estate's Discounters* plus, *Real Estate Dough: Your Recipe for Real Estate Success,* and the game that teaches real estate negotiating—Real Estate Dough-Negotiation. www.RealEstateCoach.com

From Negotiation Trainers for Realtors®

"Tim Burrell's *Create a Great Deal* is the best negotiation book ever written for real estate professionals. It is thorough, enlightening, and full of outstanding negotiation advice. Agents who implement Tim's approaches and techniques will become exceptional negotiators not only in real estate, but in non-real estate negotiations as well."

— **Tom Hayman**, Owner/CEO of Negotiation Expertise, LLC, and author of the top negotiation training course in real estate, "Certified Negotiation Expert (CNE®) Designation Course for Real Estate Professionals." www.NegotiationExpertise.com

From Negotiation Professionals and Speakers

"William Shatner doesn't really get negotiation. But Tim Burrell does. His new book *Create a Great Deal* applies down-to-earth, adult negotiation strategies and principles to the real estate field. For real estate professionals and those buying or selling property it is a definite `buy it and read it' book. I love it...."

— **Phil Marcus, Esq.**, 35-year Washington D.C. area litigation and business lawyer, presenter of the "Zen and the Art of Negotiation" seminars and author of a forthcoming book by the same name. www.NegotiationPro.com

From Top Realtors® in the Luxury Market

"The ability to negotiate is very important in the luxury home market. Most upper tier buyers and sellers are savvy negotiators, so a Realtor® who works this segment of the market needs to demonstrate mastery of the art of real estate negotiating. Being an adept negotiator will put you in the inner circle of their valued advisors and help you maintain them as clients for life. Tim Burrell's book gives you the tools you need to work in any market, including the luxury market."

— **Jo Ellen Nash**, CRS, serving the Luxury Markets of Naples, Fl and Vail, CO, Founding Guild Member, Institute for Luxury Home Marketing, Star Power Star, CyberStar®. www.NashVail.com and www.NashNaples.com

"Tim Burrell has been developing quality material on negotiating for years, gaining tips from some of the top negotiating real estate agents in the country. He's made presentations to real estate groups, moderated panels, and arranged mock negotiations. This book is a compilation of the best of the best on negotiating, a critical skill for the successful real estate agent. Good negotiating skills help clients get better results—receiving more as a seller, and paying less as a buyer. Further, in many cases, good negotiating skills can mean the difference between closing a sale and losing a property. I highly recommend this book for agents who want to be more successful for themselves and for their clients."

— **Sharon Simms**, CIPS CRS CLHMS ABR CRB RSPS, instructor for the Certified Luxury Home Marketing Specialist course, ALVA International, Inc., St. Petersburg, Florida. www.SSimms.com

From Top Realtors in the Bank Owned (REO) Market

"This book is very informative and well written and offers real life successful negotiation scenarios, instead of the usual hype. It should be endorsed by every real estate organization, because Realtors® need this talent to succeed."

— **Tom Moon**, Founder of ReoBroker.com, former #1 agent Nationwide for ERA, top agent in Orange County, CA for 2007 and #2 for 2008, Director REOMAC, over $150 Million in sales in 2008. www.REObroker.com

From Top Producing Agents Across America

"Of the many skills a good Realtor® needs to master, none is no more important than negotiating. All the work to get a listing or to pick up a buyer is for naught if you don't have the skills necessary to get you to the finish line. Tim shows you not just how to get to the finish line but well beyond that line."

> — **Rob Levy**, CRS, Star Power Star, CyberStar®, Portland Oregon's top Realtor® with over 20 years experience, #63 worldwide for Prudential Real Estate. www.RobLevy.com

"When Tim and I were at the same firm, he taught me a great deal about negotiating. Now, this book shares his insight with Realtors® everywhere. You will learn how to make more sales, have them go together better and close more easily, all the while working more smoothly with the other Realtors®. You need this book in today's market."

> — **Jim Allen**, Raleigh, North Carolina, #5 agent nationwide for Coldwell Banker, former #2 agent nationwide for Prudential. www.JimAllen.com

"With the troubled real estate market, Realtors® need to take advantage of every opportunity to make a sale. With the techniques that Tim teaches, Realtors® will be able to make more clients happy, while they make more sales. Besides that, this book will teach you to get the best deal for your client while you make everyone feel that they've won."

> — **Cheryl Scott Daniels**, CRS, CyberStar, Westport, CT. #3 ERA broker team in the USA, Realtor of the Year 1993 and 2002. www.CSDGroup.com

"Being a successful negotiator is what the clients of today expect in a Realtor®. Negotiating is a skill that is learned. Don't learn it the hard way. Tim's book captures all the essential elements you need to learn to be a successful negotiator!"

> — **Pat Wattam**, CRS, Star Power Star, CyberStar®, Baton Rouge, LA. with over 25 years experience and consistently the Number 1 RE/MAX Team in Baton Rouge. www.PatWattam.com

"This is a must-read for any real estate agent who plans to succeed. Tim Burrell has effectively presented the skills necessary to thrive in the real estate market. Agents must know how to increase the number of potential sales though negotiating. This real estate-specific look at negotiating will show you how to do it."

— **Darryl Baskin**, CyberStar®, one of the top agents in Tulsa, OK, weekly radio talk show host, and television talent for "The Future of Real Estate." www.DarrylBaskin.com

"With the difficult market in Florida, Realtors® need to succeed with every opportunity to make a sale. Particularly in today's market, negotiating talent is essential for putting the sale together and negotiating it again and again all the way to closing. Tim Burrell's book teaches the negotiating skills you will need to not only make more sales, but to get a better agreement for your clients. Learn what Tim can teach you so that you can enjoy the real estate profession more."

— **Brett Ellis**, CRS, Star Power Star, CyberStar®, RE/MAX Hall of Fame, Speaker RE/MAX International Conventions, #1 sales Team, Lee County, FL. www.TopAgent.com

"Sellers want the highest dollar for their property. Buyers want the highest value for the lowest dollar. Successful transactions—deals that close—demand skillful negotiations. Too often, real estate agents confuse negotiation with confrontation. Learn the difference. Tim Burrell's book teaches how to negotiate better, make more clients happy and make more sales close."

— **Kathy Drewien**, CRS, CyberStar®, premier Atlanta, GA Realtor®, featured on the June '07 cover "Generations Relations" issue of CRS Magazine, real estate technology specialist. www.AtlantaRelo.com

"I was so fortunate to read the first draft of Tim's book *Create A Great Deal*. The title is perfect. During my review I was in the middle of several transactions and used Tim's negotiating techniques. His "tools" allowed me to make the best deals for my clients. Tim gives the best advice and makes this a Win-win for all...especially the Real Estate agent!"

— **Margaret Rome**, CRS, CyberStar®, author of *Real Estate the Rome Way*, one of the top Realtors® in Baltimore, MD. www.HomeRome.com

"Tim Burrell's book, *Create A Great Deal*, teaches negotiating in the best manner possible, by using stories and personal examples. We Realtors® relate to people and the best way for us to understand and remember concepts, tools and principles is to relate them to stories. I highly recommend this book to everyone in the real estate business as we can all benefit from better negotiating skills."

— **Beth McKinney**, CRS, Star Power Star, CyberStar®, RE/MAX Hall of Fame, top agent for RE/MAX UNITED in Cary, North Carolina. www.BudnBeth.com

Create
A Great Deal

The Art of Real Estate Negotiating

Tim Burrell

The Silloway Press

Columbia, MD

Published by The Silloway Press, Columbia, Maryland.

Cover design by Judy Burrell
Printed in the United States of America

Burrell, Tim. Create a Great Deal: The Art of Real Estate Negotiation/
Tim Burrell

  LCCN: 2009921604
  ISBN-13: 978-0-9802057-0-1
  ISBN-10: 0-9802057-0-0

The Silloway Press, 9437 Clocktower Lane, Columbia, MD 21046
  301-335-9368 – CAGD@SillowayPress.com - http://SillowayPress.com

This book is dedicated to Judy Burrell, my wife, who taught me the value of negotiating in elementary school, then taught me the joy of love and family, and continues to delight me as we live and work together.

CONTENTS

Introduction

This book has been developing over a long, long time. It started when I lost a major negotiation in the fourth grade to a beautiful, blonde-haired girl with big blue eyes. She used a technique that I didn't learn until decades later to get the best rock in my rock collection in return for a lesser one and the promise that there might be another trade in the future. I became interested in the art of negotiating right then, as I did not get what I deserved: I got less because I did not know how to negotiate. By the way, there were other trades with that beautiful girl. We were married in 1969, and our relationship is the best thing in my life.

The most difficult part about a real estate sale is occasionally the other agent. Yes, there are difficult customers, stressful situations, and sudden problems. But if you and the other agent can work well together, the experience can be professional and produce an expertly choreographed dance. If you and the other agent cannot mesh, it gets ugly.

This is where negotiating skills come in. When both agents have it, you dance well together. When one has it and the other doesn't, you may be able to lead and follow well enough to get both of you through it semi-gracefully. When neither has any of this training, you stumble, step on each other's feet, and occasionally fall as the deal suffers or falls apart.

This book hopes to be a part of improving the lives of real estate agents and the experiences that their customers have. The best way to use this book is to look over the chapters and think about where you are in the stages of learning and experience. You will get the most out of it by reading it from cover to cover, but a focus on the principles, rules, tools, and techniques will get you the most improvement for the least effort. Others may need to know what to do right now in negotiating a listing commission, a repair issue, a buyer's agency agreement, or a multiple offer situation. There are chapters that will guide you specifically in those situations. Other agents may get the most out of understanding the structure of negotiations, and others may benefit the most from learning to create a game plan that will take them through the entire process. Most real estate agents want to learn the tricks, i.e. to get a silver bullet that gets results. While the chapter on tricks is fun, if you understand the principles, follow the rules in this book, acquire the right tools for the negotiating trade and do the preparation to give yourself the most knowledge possible, you will get better results than what you can get from any clever maneuver. So, get the most out of this book by concentrating on what is the most useful to you.

Buying a house is a decision that is based more on emotion than logic. It is a transaction with an enormous effect on a family that deals with amounts of money that are huge for most buyers and sellers. By developing your talent to negotiate well in these emotional, high pressure situations, you can greatly improve your clients' lives.

This book is a great start to developing your negotiating skills, as it puts you in touch with all the ideas you need to succeed. At the end of the book, you will be invited to continue your development by joining the Real Estate Negotiating Institute at **www.CreateAGreatDeal.com**.

If more agents improve their abilities in this art, we can create a great deal—not only by creating one great deal at a time, but also by creating a great deal of respect for our profession.

CHAPTER 1

THE ANATOMY OF REAL ESTATE NEGOTIATIONS

This book will teach you the skills you will need to negotiate throughout all the stages of a real estate transaction. One of your first negotiations will be with a real estate firm to get into the practice of representing clients. Next you will start the process of a sale by negotiating with the client. Then you will negotiate with the seller over the terms of the listing, your commission, and the price of the house and other aspects of marketing the home. Or you will negotiate a buyer's agency contract with a potential purchaser.

Next you will negotiate with your counterpart—the other real estate agent—when there is some interest in a property. The initial conversations about the property can frame the future negotiations. How you start, what kind of initial offer is made, and how you react to that offer can have a major impact on the success, or failure, of the sale. Then you will work through offers, counter-offers, and the final resolution of an agreement.

After that, you will negotiate your way to closing. The repair issues will constitute a full round of negotiations, as you will need to reach an agreement on the condition of the property and what will be done to make the condition satisfactory to the buyer. The dynamics of the sale will change from the initial negotiations to the ones that move toward closing.

Right at the closing, there will be another group of negotiations over the last minute issues that frequently arise, as well as the condition of the property during the walk through. Being able to gracefully hold a sale together at the finish is the difference between getting paid for all your work, or coming close with no compensation.

Finally, there will even be negotiations after closing, from discoveries about the condition of the property to follow-ups on uncompleted promises and dealing with warranty issues. As you can see, the ability to negotiate is the most important skill for a real estate agent to have, because it is used throughout the entire process.

There is one oddity of the process of real estate negotiating: You have more of an interest in a successful outcome and avoiding a disastrous outcome than your client does. If the sale comes together and closes, you get paid. If it goes horribly and the client finds another agent, you don't get paid on this transaction—or get any future business from that client. So, learn to negotiate well.

What Makes a Good Negotiator?

Now that you have seen how negotiating fits into each step of a sale, you need to focus on what it takes to develop your negotiating talent. Most Americans do not start out as good negotiators. Why? They do not know the principles, understand the rules, or have the tools to negotiate well. Also, they think that negotiations are confrontational, where one side wins and the other side loses. So they fear it, and the stress makes the experience unpleasant.

In the Internet Age, where everyone has access to all the listings and an abundance of information, your talent as a negotiator may be the most important skill you possess. Real estate agents cannot avoid negotiating if they want to earn a living. Therefore, developing certain personal skills will let you negotiate better and enjoy the process. Luckily for you, negotiators are made, not born, so let's start the process.

I do not know if I agree with Ed Brodow in *Negotiation Boot Camp* when he says that the TV detective Columbo is the consummate negotiator. He cites Columbo as the model because:

- he keeps his ego in check;
- he asks an abundance of questions;
- he listens well;
- he is a problem solver;
- he is reasonable in his approach;
- he is humble;
- he aims to find the truth;
- he does not have a goal of winning the battle of egos.

There is a lot to be said for Columbo as a role model, but you might want to develop your own best example after reviewing the following characteristics of a good negotiator.

A good negotiator is reliable and trustworthy.

Do what you say you are going to do so your clients, and especially your counterpart will be able to trust that you will follow through, even if that follow through is not positive for your counterpart. In addition, do not state something as fact unless you are personally sure it is true, because well-meaning clients will give you incorrect information that will damage your credibility. Your reputation for honesty and integrity with other real estate agents is critical, as it affects how they treat you and your clients. Earning this reputation in the real estate community will take time; you cannot just say, "Trust me," as that phrase usually causes an alarm to go off in most negotiator's heads.

When I was just starting in the profession, I presented an offer to a well-established real estate agent who headed a small real estate firm in Palos Verdes Estates, California. I believed him when he said there were other offers coming in on the property, and I got my clients to improve their offer to beat the competition. I reacted too quickly: There were never other offers. The next time I presented an offer to him, I heard the same claim. This time, I waited for a response from his clients. When no other offers came in, I did not believe anything else he told me. Thereafter, when I presented offers, I had to double-check everything he represented before I relayed anything to my clients. Today, his firm is still in business, but he is not.

A good negotiator is thoroughly prepared and completely aware.

Know the market, the property, your client's issues, the other party's issues, as well as the personalities and negotiating styles of everyone involved in any transaction.

"Genius is 1 percent inspiration and 99 percent perspiration," according to Thomas Edison.

Developing this awareness of the people, real estate, and the market around you will help you pick up every signal you can and trust your senses, so you can see through the games other people play. In *Secrets of Winning the Real Estate Negotiation Game*, Seth Weissman and Ned Blumenthal refer to the combination of these two forms of awareness as being "consciously detached." I like the way detachment implies that you are above the battle. However, I prefer the term used by athletes when they are really on their game. They refer to it as being "in the zone"—when they feel that not only are they performing at a high level but also they are keenly aware of all of the moves going on around them.

An additional, very important part of knowledge you need is to know yourself. You should know your personality type and what your strengths and weaknesses are. Understand your emotions: Which ones help? Which ones get you into trouble? (I have the classic Irish temper. It gives me lots of energy, but it has also given me lots of trouble.) When you know the kinds of filters you have on reality, you are better able to handle all the information you need to understand. Do not dwell on this, as you want to be conscious of yourself, but not so self conscious that you focus too much on yourself and do not focus enough on paying attention to everyone and everything in the process.

Contrary to popular belief, negotiating success is more about listening and less about talking. Most people believe great negotiators are smooth talkers. The best negotiators are great listeners.

A good negotiator sets reasonable expectations.

Before you start helping clients buy or sell, set realistic expectations. Is it realistic to think that there is a perfect house? No, so do not lead the clients to expect that they will get one. Is it realistic to sell a house well above market value? No, selling a house far above the market value means that it will not appraise, which means that the sale will not close.

Repeat this mantra: "I sell real estate, I don't do magic." As long as your clients expect something that is within the range of possibility, you have a chance of pleasing them. A way to help set this up is to get clients to establish realistic goals. A real estate agent who exceeds those goals has a client for life and an abundance of referrals. The ultimate mistake in setting expectations is a guarantee. Never guarantee anything, unless you also want to follow up with "and if it does not happen that way, I will pay the difference out of my pocket."

My daughter, Laurie Hughes, and I represented Paul and Brenda, buyers who were moving to Rancho Palos Verdes, California, from San Jose. They were buying when the market was in a seller's frenzy; nearly every home had multiple offers and most homes sold over the asking price. We explained this to the family so they would understand that we could not guarantee they would be the successful bidder on any one house. We had them choose two houses that they liked and put in offers on both of them, after determining that there were no other offers on either house. We told each listing agent that we had an offer on another house, and the first one to get accepted would be the one we would purchase.

You have to present this forcefully enough, with plenty of detail on the other house you are working on, so that the listing agent believes you. Also, you have to have good credibility in your marketplace to be able to be convincing. We did not give the listing agents time to develop multiple offers from other potential buyers who had seen the house, so they had to consider our offer, which was under the asking price. One agent convinced their sellers to accept our offer, while the other agent did not get back to us within the time we had provided. It happened that the offer that was accepted was on the house our clients liked better.

The buyers started the process with realistic expectations: that it would be hard to get any house. Since they had hired a good negotiator, they ended up getting the house they wanted for less than the asking price in a market where everyone else was paying above the asking price. What does this do for you as a real estate agent? It gets you respect and loyalty.

During the escrow on this property, there was a problem with a drain line that the seller refused to fix, as they were a little annoyed that they had accepted such a low price. My daughter and I planned to have it fixed for our clients and pay for it with some of our commission, because the commission on a million dollar house can easily cover the cost of a little plumbing. The buyer, who was not native to the U.S., was just learning American slang. This incident gave him the opportunity to use a new idiom. He said, "I have just learned the right phrase for that: 'No way in Hell'—is that the right term?!" He was so happy with our efforts at negotiating that he would not let us take less than our full commission, and he was glad to pay for that item himself just to show his appreciation.

A good negotiator is creative.

An important skill is learning to free your mind so that you can come up with creative solutions. Mental dexterity is critical when you reach an impasse. Don't "think outside the box"; instead, think of a wide range of ideas and let your mind wander to parallel experiences in other worlds that might let the problem solve itself.

This first principle is best explained by "changing the framework" or the terms. If you face a situation where zebras are prohibited, see if you can change the terminology so that your zebra becomes a striped horse.

I sold a property in Clayton, North Carolina, that was a "short sale,"—the proceeds of the sale would not be enough to pay off the loans and judgments on the property. (One of the lend-

ers was Wells Fargo, and they were represented by an excellent loss mitigation negotiator, Ms. Davenport. I represented both the buyer and the seller, so I was able to understand what everyone involved wanted from the sale.) Abandoned for months, the house was not in good condition, and the buyer wanted to have a home warranty to lessen the risk of repairs after the sale. The lender insisted that the house be sold "as is" and that no warranties whatsoever could be allowed. (Wells Fargo had had the unfortunate experience of being involved in an "as is" sale where a home warranty was provided. That warranty made a court decide the sale was not completely "as is," so the buyer could contest the condition of the property after the sale.)

This first-time homebuyer did not have the cash to pay for unforeseen repairs, which a home warranty would cover. The lender did not want to be vulnerable to the argument that providing any type of warranty opened them up to future litigation. During the discussions, we shifted the focus to the fact that what was really at stake was the amount of $495 to pay for the warranty. Once the framework of the problem changed, the solution became apparent. Wells Fargo would allow the seller to pay an additional $495 toward the buyer's closing costs so the buyer would have $495 additional cash on hand when the sale closed and could purchase the warranty. Thus the warranty became a closing cost. Everyone got what they needed.

Another way to think about freeing your mind is that if you find yourself at an impasse, see if you can change the rules of the game to eliminate the problem. Many issues in real estate sales arise from procedural requirements, and if you can change the procedure, you can eliminate the problem. Since you are dealing with highly regulated banks, governmental agencies that record documents, attorneys, and escrow officers that close sales only by the book, it may seem to be an impossible situation.

In California, my team represented a buyer who was a proofreader for a pharmaceutical company, a man of high principles who was a stickler for details. At the escrow, everything was going well until the last loan document, which required a notary's seal. The law required that a notary get the thumbprint of the person whose signature is being validated. This buyer felt that the government was intruding too far into his life. He would not put his thumbprint in the notary's book.

My father was this buyer's agent. He called me from the escrow office with the problem. My first question: What witness protection program was the buyer in, so that he would not let the notary have his thumbprint? After talking with the buyer, it was clear that was not the problem. I tried to explain the Fourth Amendment as this was not the government interfering with his privacy, with no effect. I tried to see if we could get it notarized in a different manner, also with no luck. Meanwhile, the buyer's wife was furious, saying that she and the children would be out in the street because their lease was ending at their present residence, and she wanted to buy this house. He would not budge.

So, I focused on how we could change the procedural requirements. For sales in North Carolina, we frequently send documents to buyers or sellers in other states and other countries to be signed, notarized, and returned. The notary does not have to comply with North Carolina laws, just the laws of the state where the documents are being signed.

I called George Durkin, a real estate agent in Las Vegas, and asked him if the notary provisions in Nevada required a thumbprint. They did not. There are dozens of flights from Los Angeles to Las Vegas every day, with low fares. My father got the documents that needed to be signed and sent the buyer to the airport for a flight to Las Vegas and a notary who had the experience to be sure all the papers were properly signed. In a few hours, the buyer came back with the documents signed and notarized—and with his principles intact. I disagreed with his position, but I had to respect his feelings. So, changing the procedure to one he could live with let the sale close smoothly, and gave his wife a wonderful story to tell about the character she married instead of giving her grounds for divorce.

If you have enough experience to look at a problem from a fresh perspective, and enough sense to apply the fact that the rules change depending on where you are, <u>you can solve procedural stalemates by changing the procedure.</u>

A good negotiator is considerate of the counterpart's personality and negotiating style.

If you speak English as your native language, but also speak French fluently, and your counterpart speaks French as a native, but can barely get by in English, you may want to conduct the negotiations in French. The other party will be much more comfortable, and more likely to share information.

While this idea is obvious, the same concept applies to negotiating style. If you adapt your negotiating style to your counterpart's style, you can build comfort and trust. If you are dealing with a detailed, analytical person who thinks visually, give them tons of details in pictures and plenty of time to analyze them. When they come to the right conclusion, they will not try to renegotiate later.

The Golden Rule says to treat others the way you would like to be treated. That is fine, as far as it goes. <u>The Platinum Rule says to treat others the way that they would like to be treated</u>, <u>not the way you want to be treated</u>. So, figure out the others' style, and then adapt to them.

A good negotiator compensates for weaknesses.

A good negotiator does not reveal her weaknesses, but she does know what they are and compensates for them. Not good at math? Just bring a calculator. Have a hard time reviewing detailed agreements? Just study the standard forms well in advance of your need to use them. Have a poor memory? Take lots of notes and review them before your meeting or phone call. Since a good negotiator will take advantage of the weaknesses of the others in the negotiations, a good negotiator will also need to be sure to compensate for any personal failings.

No matter how weak your position, never let them see you sweat. When Miss USA trips on her high heels at the Miss Universe Pageant, she gets up immediately with a perfect smile and hopes her deodorant is working. I think of negotiating like a dance. My favorite line about dancing/negotiating is from the movie *Scent of a Woman*: "If you make a mistake and get tangled up, you just Tango on."

A good negotiator asserts the client's position.

Your primary objective is to sell your client's position. Present your client's "needs" and try to get their "wants" in a manner that makes them clear to your counterparts.

At the same time, <u>challenge any position that interferes with getting your client's needs and wants met</u>. This is not to say be aggressive, but rather to be assertive. To do this, you do not have to change your character, just your behavior. Since the object is to reach an agreement that meets your client's needs, you need to speak up and assert those needs. When you are presented with a contrary position, acknowledge that position, then present your position. Remember, if you do not ask, you do not get.

A good negotiator is schooled in all types of negotiations.

Collaborative negotiations (Win-win) end up with more valuable transactions, by increasing the value of what each party gets. For example, in collaborative negotiations, the information you share can make the entire transaction more valuable and lead to a better agreement. However, there are negotiations where you can only use win-lose. Using the same example, information you share in a win-lose negotiation is frequently used against you and results in a worse result for your client. You will learn to recognize all the types of negotiations, how to work in each one, and when to switch from one to the other in chapter three.

A good negotiator is guided by communication with the clients.

Your clients need to be aware of what you know: Knowledge is power. When you give your clients choices, and explain the advantages and disadvantages of each choice, they will make the right choice. If they are missing critical information, they will come to the wrong conclusion.

Telling your client bad news quickly is particularly important. If they are going to be upset about the bad news, do not compound it by making them even angrier that they could have known about it earlier and might have acted differently in the interim if they had known the bad news.

Similarly, you need to get critical information from your client.

> *Early in my career, I had a client who presented an excellent façade of being financially able to weather a tough real estate market, as he resisted my efforts to reduce the price of his listing in order to get it sold. When I saw the foreclosure notice on his property in the paper, we had to drop the price dramatically, since the rest of the real estate world now knew he was in financial distress. If I had known the true financial status earlier, we could have sold the property for more money, and sold it more gracefully. I should have asked more questions, listened better, and picked up other signs of distress, such as his wife's body language when I came to visit the house.*

You cannot communicate too much with a client, because they need to be involved in every step of the process, as it is their interests and goals that guide the process.

A good negotiator asks for more than she expects to get.

While you want to keep your request within the range of plausibility, open the negotiations by asking for more than you expect to get. First, you just might get it. Second, it gives you something to give up, so that the other side feels like your concessions are a gain for them. Third, your counterpart perceives you as ending up in a position that is better for them than the opening position, which makes the end result feel more valuable. Fourth, it gives you a tool to avoid a deadlock, as you have something to give up if the other side gets stuck on a particular position. Finally, it gives you the ability to make major concessions, which causes your counterpart to feel favorably toward you. In other words, you seem like a much nicer person if you show major movement in your position in response to their counter offers.

However, you do not want to start with a ridiculous offer. Stay within the range that you can reasonably defend, preferably with some comparable values or other independent validation. If you insult the other party, you will either have no negotiations at all, or you will have to apologize during the course of the negotiations, with a worse result than if you had started at a reasonable place.

A good negotiator can analyze every experience.

When you put a sale together, and again after you close the sale, learn from it. Go over what you did, evaluate how well it worked, and imagine what could have worked better. Most major businesses use this concept of Continuous Improvement to make their processes better. You should do the same. The same issues repeat themselves in real estate sales. Learning from them will improve your performance every time an issue arises and will increase your skill in the art of negotiations.

Some of these skills you can learn from a book. If you are lucky, you can be an apprentice or team member to a master negotiator, as it is easier to pick it up by having a mentor. The mentor will have analyzed many performances, and you can see the results. If you have a mentor, discuss each negotiation so that you can pick apart the things you did well, pick up on the things you did poorly, and develop a way to improve.

If you do not have a mentor, you may want to join the Real Estate Negotiating Institute at **www.CreateAGreatDeal. com**, as it can be your online mentor.

Part of the review is to point out the successes to your client. Most people remember the first thing and the last thing that happened in a transaction. If the last thing is a discussion of the parts that went well, you will improve your relationship.

There is one caution to the use of this process. Do not get "analysis paralysis." Just do it. You will not do it perfectly, ever. So, give yourself permission to make mistakes, because you will. Also, realize that there is almost never a clearly right way or wrong way to proceed. So just try something and see what happens, then adjust. If the sale closes and everyone walks away happy, you did well, even if you could have done better. Next time, you will do better.

A good negotiator is guided by practice, practice, and more practice.

Lawyers read the cases, but they only learn the craft by practicing. Surgeons study the literature, but skill comes from doing operations.

Negotiation is an art, not a science. With enough transactions and enough analysis, you will develop a feel for what to do in any situation. If you are lucky enough to have a mentor, you will pick up some of the mentor's feel for the situation and shorten your learning curve by watching what your mentor does.

Take these ideas, rehearse them with a friend, role play with colleagues, then use them in real life by practicing on items that do not matter, like negotiating the price with a sales clerk at a store. Analyze your triumphs and tragedies. Read about others' experiences and share yours at **www.CreateAGreatDeal.com.** Then get better and better.

Now that you know what makes a great negotiator, you need to learn the language of negotiations so that new concepts can stretch your ability.

Chapter 2

Understanding the Language of Negotiations

There are certain major ideas in negotiating that are vital for you to understand in order for you to be successful. The definition of some terms will help you be more comfortable with the ideas behind negotiating. Just reading about these terms and concepts will broaden your thinking and give you ideas you can use in your next sale. Once you fully understand them, you can use them to your—and your clients'—advantage.

Terms

Negotiating

We could go through all sorts of scholarly definitions of negotiating, but let's get right to what works in this context. Negotiating is exchanging information, ideas, and proposals concerning real estate to accomplish the purchase and sale of real property. While there are many more definitions of negotiating in the Appendix, some of the more interesting ones merit a mention here.

One of my favorites is from George Ross in *Trump Style Negotiations*: "I tell my students that negotiation is a process in which people learn to accept an available compromise as a satisfactory substitute for that which they thought they really wanted." He is right; you are getting the parties to adjust to a compromise that is a reasonable facsimile of their original goal.

In *Negotiation Boot Camp*, Ed Brodow says "Negotiation is the process of overcoming obstacles in order to reach agreement." You have to make it past the stumbling blocks to get to a deal. Mr. Brodow makes an excellent point when he explains that negotiating is about collaborating, not just about winning.

"Negotiating is the commerce of information for ultimate gain," according to Ronald Shapiro and Mark Jankowski in *The Power of Nice*. Their point is that the commerce is not the exchange of goods, but the exchange of information that creates the gain by trading what you know for what you need to know.

Counterpart

Many negotiators refer to the person they are negotiating with as the other side, an adversary or an opponent. This creates a confrontational mindset, which steers you toward a win-lose negotiating style. The term "counterpart" provides a better reference and gets you thinking about common goals, because both sides in real estate sales want the same result: to put the sale together.

Framing

Framing is setting up the perspective from which you want people to look at a subject. Is the glass half-full? It is if you want to emphasize abundance. Or is it half-empty? Yes, if you want to emphasize scarcity. Or is it that "the glass is too big"? Yes, if you want to emphasize that you can adjust other factors to reach a better result.

The best way to frame an issue is by analogy, i.e. by tying into a person's pre-existing mental models. So, if you refer to your counterpart's proposal as a shakedown, the image of a robbery sets your client up to refuse it. If you refer to the counterpart's proposal as a gift on a silver platter, your client will be inclined to accept it.

The Anchor

In general, an anchor is a reference point from which adjustments are made. Most often an anchor is created by the starting point in negotiations, such as the first offer, which has a psychological effect on what each side believes is a possible outcome to the negotiations. Most of the time, the price at which a home is listed in the Multiple Listing Service is an anchor.

When you have a good idea of the price at which your counterpart would walk away from the negotiations, you may want to try to anchor the negotiations with an offer that is favorable to you. For example, you know the list price, but the listing agent says they are extremely flexible. If you can find out what offers they have rejected, you can get an idea of their walk-away price. Then, you can make your first offer to anchor the negotiations around a point that is favorable to you, i.e. start low. <u>If you do not have any idea of the counterpart's walk-away price, it may be better to let your counterpart make the first move</u>.

Winner's Curse

Whenever you make a deal, you are cursed with the thought that you could have gotten a better deal. This idea is particularly true if your counterpart accepts your first offer. We will discuss later how to slowly accept a first offer, with certain reservations, to try to counteract the winner's curse. Buyer's remorse is a type of winner's curse.

Renegotiations

After a deal is reached, one party wants to change one term of the deal. In the event that this happens after new information is discovered, it may feel more acceptable. For example, the home inspection reveals foundation problems that no one knew about, so you may want to reopen negotiations to provide an allowance for the repair of the foundation. On the other hand, if one party wants to counteract their case of winner's curse by trying to get a better deal, you may want to respond that if they want to reopen negotiations on one term, that reopens negotiations on all terms, as the deal is an integrated sum of many parts. If the renegotiating party decides to leave the deal alone, they were just testing you. If they want to reopen negotiations anyway, see what other choices you have and consider the emotional joy of walking away from someone who does not honor their word.

Structural Impediments and Spoilers

A structural impediment is something that is blocking negotiations, i.e. a problem with the way the deal is structured that prevents agreement. The best examples are having an essential party to the process missing. For example, the husband of a couple is in town looking at homes and finds one he loves. Without his wife's involvement, it is difficult to proceed with a purchase agreement.

Spoilers can also be structural impediments. Spoilers are parties that are preventing an agreement. The best example is a parent of a first-time home buyer, particularly the father of a young lady. A parent who has not participated in the selection process has not seen what is available and what the choices are. If the parent looks only at the home the child has selected, the normal response is for the parent to try to show how much smarter they are than the child and the real estate agent by finding major flaws with the purchase. The solution: If the parent is an essential part of the decision-making process, make them go through the entire process and look at every home, or at least look at a range of homes, to see what choices are available.

> *Chris Laurence, a real estate agent in Front Royal, Virginia, tells a story of how to deal with a spoiler. "I had a buyer client who was fresh out of law school, whose father was a long-term lawyer. The father, who was physically imposing with an overbearing personality, wanted to see a copy of the contract. He proceeded to cross out large paragraphs, re-write other parts, and generally re-create his own document. After a half-hour of this nonsense, I told him that the contract was drawn up by the Virginia Association of real estate agents as a fair document to both parties and it was tried and tested. I explained that I would not move forward unless his son used the standard agreement. It seemed no one had stood up to him like that before, as he became very flustered and then said to his son, 'You're on your own, son'! His son 'fired' him and went ahead without any changes."*

Exploding Offer

An exploding offer is one that goes away, typically due to a time limit. If you want a quick reaction from your counterpart, so they cannot shop your offer with other potential buyers, place a short time limit for their acceptance. Just like a time bomb, when the time expires, the offer explodes.

Restrictive, or Closed, Questions

A closed question can be answered by either "yes" or "no." In more general terms, it is a question that seeks a specific piece of information. The best time to use this type of question is to confirm an understanding, so that all parties are clear on where they stand, because everyone hears the short answer of "yes" or "no." "Do we have an agreement on the price at $375,000?" The answer will make it clear.

Open-Ended Questions

Real Estate Trainer Floyd Wickman calls these "Wopen" questions, because most of them start with a W: Who, what, where, when, why, and (breaking the rule by ending with a w) how. In lawyer's terms, they are not leading questions, as they let the responder go wherever they want. If you want to find out your counterpart's concerns, interests, and deal points, ask open-ended questions. Then, follow up with "What will (insert their answer) do for you?" If you want to understand better, follow the answer to that question with "How is that important to you?" You can keep pursuing this line of questioning until you reach the real motivation behind any issue.

Watch out for "why": If you have a teenage child, you know the effects of starting a question with "why"—and if you have a two year old, you know what it's like to be on the receiving end of it! Most people react defensively to "why," as it sounds like you are judging them. They try to explain themselves and defend what they sense is an attack on their position. Instead of using this intimidating term, use some of the other open questions. Instead of "Why is that important?" try "What makes that important?"

Concepts

Implicit Needs are more important than Explicit Needs

Explicit needs are the ones that a party to negotiations expresses, e.g., a good price, a certain number of bedrooms, particular financing, and various characteristics of the property. Implicit needs are the ones the party really feels but rarely expresses openly. In *The Only Negotiating Guide You'll Ever Need*, Peter B. Stark and Jane Flaherty give a partial list of implicit needs:

- to be liked or loved
- to trust and be trusted
- to be respected
- to be right
- to look good in someone else's eyes
- to be "better" or have authority
- to get a good deal
- to feel listened to
- to be recognized
- to appear intelligent
- to win, regardless of how small the deal point
- to have a relationship

For example, most people want to be respected and given credit for being a smart investor. If they get that feeling out of a sale, they are satisfied. <u>You will find that implicit needs are much more important in determining the outcome of a negotiation than the explicit needs</u>.

Active Listening

Active listening involves not just listening, but also being clear to your counterpart that you hear what they are saying. Active listening is characterized by undivided attention, eye contact with the speaker, inviting body language, and asking follow-up questions—an easy form of which is, "Let me be sure I understand what you mean..."; then paraphrase what the speaker said. <u>Another way to show you understand the speaker is to repeat back what you've heard</u>, for example, that it's important to them to keep the dining room chandelier that has been in the family for generations. Then you can suggest: "Since your grandfather's chandelier does not stay with the house, should we replace it before we put the home on the market?" to show that you are following their story. If you want to get more creative, paraphrase what was said incorrectly so that the speaker can correct your misstatement, a technique that works well with "control freaks" as the more they correct you, the happier they are.

One way to get the speaker to continue with their thought is to repeat back the last part of what they said, then make some affirming comment. For example, you could say, "Your grandfather bought this chandelier...great!" Then be quiet and let the speaker continue. If the speaker is discussing something painful, repeating back what they said followed by "ouch" works wonders.

Unfortunately, many real estate agents are so busy thinking of what they are going to say next that they do not listen well. This is one of the biggest mistakes in negotiating. Don't just wait for your turn to talk, listen actively.

Interrupting is another flaw in many agents' listening technique. If your counterpart is about to disclose their needs or wants, or even more importantly, if they are about to agree with you, do not stop their train of thought. If you stop it, you will never know what you missed. This was hard for me to learn, as I can figure out where a slow talker is going, and I used to try to help them get there. I had to learn how to sit back from my grandchildren. If I jump in to help them get something done, it is less satisfying to them. Let your counterpart tell you their entire story herself; it will make the negotiations go more smoothly.

Auction Effect

Bidders frequently get carried away at auctions, getting caught up in the moment and bidding too much because they want to beat the other bidders. If you can get several bidders going for your property, you might have the joy of hearing a wife tell her husband, "George, don't you let them get my home" as she urges him to throw reason to the wind and bid whatever it takes to win. The implicit need to dominate the competition and look good in a spouse's eyes causes the bidding to exceed the appropriate value. Auctions are a wonderful way to negotiate, if you can get the bidding started and feed the fire until the auction effect kicks in.

Other Choice, or BATNA

The Best Alternative to Negotiated Agreement (BATNA) is a term developed in *Getting to Yes* by Roger Fisher and William Ury. In other words, what is your best course of action if you do not reach this deal? It is an important idea, as it helps you know whether the deal you are working on makes sense or whether you would be better off walking away and taking the alternative. I prefer the term "Other Choice," because it is easier to understand, not to mention easier to pronounce.

External Standards or Fairness

Most people say they want to reach a deal that is fair and reasonable. I have dealt with a lot of people who say that, but they will not accept a fair and reasonable deal. Be aware that "talk is cheap." The best example of this are buyers who say "I do not care what the comparable values say about a home like this; I am only willing to pay this amount."

One way to show that your proposal is fair is to look at some external standard to validate your position. If you are negotiating on a house in a neighborhood that was built with standard models (what some people call "tract homes"), you can find similar homes in the same neighborhood that have sold recently. The sale prices of those homes provide an external standard to show that your proposal offering a similar price is fair. However, good negotiators will first question the criteria for the external standard that your counterpart is proposing, e.g. you should not use homes in that subdivision, you should use homes in this subdivision. Then, be prepared to show why the comparable values that are more favorable to you are more relevant and to show why those more favorable to your counterpart are less relevant. In other words, demonstrate how the homes that have prices you like are more similar to the subject home, and the homes with prices that your counterpart likes are less similar to the subject home.

Walk-Away Price

Your walk-away price is the lowest price you are prepared to consider. If the deal is only about money, it is the bottom-line price you are willing to take. Most deals are not only about money, so you need to consider other factors in arriving at the point at which you will walk away. The Harvard Business Essentials website has an interesting tool to help you analyze your walk-away price, which they call your "reservation price": www.elearning.hbsp.org/businesstools.

Zone of Possible Agreement

This is the range in which it is possible for the parties to reach agreement. If the buyer's highest price is $400,000 and the seller's lowest price is $375,000, the zone of possible agreement is $375,000 to $400,000. If there is no overlap between the walk-away prices, there will be no deal. For example, if the buyer's highest price is $375,000 and the seller's lowest price is $400,000, there is no zone of possible agreement.

Negotiator's Dilemma

In certain situations, if both sides reveal information, it is much more likely that a deal will be made or a better deal will be reached. And, in certain situations, if one side reveals information and the other does not, the side revealing the information will lose. For example, a seller has to move quickly due to a job transfer and needs a short time period between the contract and the closing. At the same time, the buyer is living in temporary housing with three small children and a dog. If both sides reveal that they need to close quickly, it is much more likely that a sale will be made with a quick closing. But, if only the buyer reveals that they are desperate to get out of their present living situation, the buyer will pay a much higher price.

The solution is to "test the waters" cautiously by revealing some information about your position and asking for some information about your counterpart's interests in return, looking for reciprocity. If you get it, proceed with more Win-win discussions. If not, switch to a win-lose posture and keep your information private.

Negotiating Power

Most of the time, negotiating power is completely subjective and stems from your belief that you have it. The most important part of negotiating power is knowledge, and we will spend an entire chapter on that. Essentially, whoever has the most choices or the best other choices has the most power. If you do not have to make a particular deal because your other choices are good, you have power. If you desperately need the deal, you do not. Discovering the pressure that your counterpart is under and eliminating pressure for your clients also increases your negotiating power. If you can find a pressure point, push on it; if you can show your counterpart that they will be worse off if they do not reach an agreement and better off if they do, you have the power of persuasion.

One of the biggest mistakes made by inexperienced negotiators is to overestimate their counterpart's strength and to underestimate their own. I love the quote from Eleanor Roosevelt that "no one can make you feel inferior without your permission." Most of us know our own weaknesses and think about them much too much, thereby giving up our power early in our careers. Instead of listening to that voice of self-doubt, think about your counterpart's weaknesses. Find your strength and find your counterpart's vulnerability. You are much more powerful than you realize. Believing in that power will go a long way to making you a successful negotiator.

Now that you have learned the language, terms and concepts of negotiating, it is time you learn the fundamental types of negotiating.

CHAPTER 3

TYPES OF NEGOTIATIONS

If the only thing you learn from this book is how to engage in collaborative negotiations, your effort will be a success. This style of negotiating is often referred to as "Win-win." This type of negotiating is so important that Keller Williams even uses it in a number of its principles.

However, you hear the term "Win-win" so often that it has become trite. The implication is that both sides win, which is not always the case. That is why I prefer the term "collaborative negotiation." "Investigative negotiating" is an even more interesting term for this style of negotiating that was coined by Deepak Malhotra and Max Bazerman in *Negotiation Genius*.

There is also, however, win-lose negotiation, which is more common in real estate, even though it does not sound as sweet.

Win-Lose Negotiation

Anyone can engage in win-lose negotiating. In this style, some negotiators believe they are doing battle, so they try to destroy the other party and ignore the fact that a destroyed party has no reason to complete the deal. They keep pushing to get concessions from the other side while trying to make as few concessions as they can. The majority of real estate agents use this style of negotiating; and if your counterpart does not engage in collaborative negotiation, you may have to use win-lose bargaining, because collaborative negotiation requires that both sides participate.

In win-lose negotiating, the parties view the transaction as having a fixed amount of something, and the more one party gets, the less the other party gets. For example, there is a fixed size of the pie; if you get a bigger piece of the pie, your counterpart gets a smaller piece. In real estate, if the price is a dollar higher, the seller gains an additional dollar and the buyer loses an additional dollar.

In this type of negotiating, you "play your cards close to your chest" and do not disclose anything important about your situation. You do not talk about why you want to buy or sell, what constraints you face, or your preferences about the issues in the negotiations. You want to let your counterpart know that you have other options to making a deal, and you want to show how good your other choice is, because it will make your counterpart more likely to let you have more of what you want. You do not indicate what your walk-away point is, because everything you say will be used against you. However, you want to learn as much as you can about your counterpart's situation, why they want to make a deal, their constraints and their preferences about the issues in the negotiations so that you can use that information against them to get more of the scarce commodity. Then, you set your first offer so that it exploits what you learn, thus anchoring the negotiations and setting a bargaining range. The best way to visualize this style is "My gain is your pain," according to *The Power of Nice* by Ron Shapiro and Mark Jankowski.

Now, if you have read other articles on negotiating, you may have seen the terms "competitive", "distributive" or "zero-sum" negotiation; these are other ways of describing win-lose negotiation.

Win-win (Collaborative) Negotiation

This type of negotiating is characterized by questioning and listening, creating trust, avoiding hostile emotions, and concentrating on ways to get mutual satisfaction. The first stage of this type of negotiating is for the parties to cooperate and exchange information, so they can create more value in the entire deal. One of the best ways to start this process is to explain that all of the parties are smarter collectively than any one of them is individually, which is a long way to say "two heads are better than one." For example, if a seller will save money by not moving twice, and the buyer can live with the seller's closing date, there is more total value to the sale with the seller's closing date. The second part of this style of negotiating is for the parties to claim their share of the value. In the example, the buyer can get a good sale price if the seller gets a favorable closing date. Thus. the process is collaborative.

To engage in this type of negotiating. it is important that each side provide useful information about their circumstances and explain why they want to make a deal by discussing their interests honestly. This is dramatically different from win-lose negotiating, where sharing information can hurt your position. In the collaborative model, each party needs to explain their preferences among the various factors in the negotiations. Both sides look to find additional terms or resources that provide value to the other side, thus enhancing the ability to make a deal. With this additional information, the goal is to create the best result for both parties by dividing up the additional value items. When you realize that your counterpart's points of value are not the same as yours, you can find something that is more important to them than it is to you. So, one of your primary efforts is to concentrate on what you can concede to your counterpart that will not damage what you want out of the agreement. In other words, you concentrate on satisfying your counterpart's needs.

Try to keep more than one issue in play in this style of negotiating. If you get down to one issue, which is frequently the price, it is hard to have both sides feel a victory. If you have a series of items, one side can have victory on some of them and the other side can feel victory on the others.

We will discuss later how "pigs grow fat but hogs get slaughtered." In collaborative negotiations, it is important not to try to take so much that there is nothing left for your counterpart. You need to leave them some dignity and some reason to complete the transaction. You may even need to put some things back on the table to accomplish this, or make some gesture of appreciation to make your counterpart feel successful in accomplishing the agreement. Some authors feel that the difference between a good negotiator and a poor negotiator is that a good negotiator exchanges minor losses for major wins.

Creating Value Through Trades

When a party to the negotiations gets something it wants by giving away something that it values less, value is created through the trade. This trade normally happens in collaborative negotiations. I had a sale where closing the sale a week earlier saved me $10,000 in penalties, and it cost the buyer only $1,000 to move up the closing date a week, so more total value was created when the buyer gave me the preferred closing date.

The type of negotiations often determines whether you can create additional value from the various interests of the parties. If you are in a win-lose format, the parties will not share their interests and put a hierarchy or relative value to the various issues to be negotiated. If you are truly in a collaboration, the parties will share their points of view and the relative worth of the various points, and a trade of different points will create more total value in the transaction, as each party can gain a concession that is more valuable to them than to their counterpart.

How to Engage in Win-Lose Negotiations

Most real estate agents engage in win-lose bargaining, so you probably already know how to do it. In this style, some negotiators believe they are doing battle, so they try to destroy the other party and ignore the fact that a destroyed party has no reason to complete the deal. In this type of negotiation, you do not reveal anything that might be used against you. You use everything revealed by your counterpart against them. You keep pushing to get concessions from the other side while trying to make as few concessions as you can. If your counterpart does not engage in collaborative negotiating, you may have to use win-lose bargaining, because collaborative negotiating requires that both sides participate.

How to Engage in Collaborative Negotiations

What are you doing?

"The best way to get what you want is to help the other side get what they want." This wonderful expression is the essence of collaborative negotiation, from *The Power of Nice* by Ron Shapiro and Mark Jankowski. The phrase "Win-win" is misleading, as you do not both win equally. You let your counterpart win on some of their needs, and you win on your most important needs. You are looking for a large WIN on your side and a small win on your counterpart's side. All the Win-win phrasing just confuses what you are trying to do, that is why I prefer to focus on collaborative negotiations and I admire the term investigative negotiations. So, it is alright if the other side has some victories, in fact, you want to make them feel victorious when it helps you get what you want.

Relative values

Collaborative negotiations require more steps and more effort than win-lose. You will first engage in discussions with your clients, to find out what their interests are, the relative strengths of the factors in the transaction, and which items they will trade off in order to get the items of higher importance.

In other words, you discover your client's concerns and interest by probing to find out what their real needs are. Next, find out your counterpart's concerns and interests, i.e. what they really want as opposed to what they say they want. The best way to find out this information is to ask open-ended questions, then listen carefully. Once you get a sense of their position, see if they are willing to trade off one item for another, so you can get a feeling for the hierarchy of the value of each item. The questions will continue throughout the process until you find out what they can live with—and what they cannot.

One of the best approaches is to ask your counterpart for pro-posed solutions. If it is their idea, they will think it is a great idea, so all you have to do is fine tune their solution. Be sure to give them credit for the solution, as it makes it much easier to sell.

If the other party is willing to tell you what issues are important to them and give you a relative hierarchy, present the same information about your position. If they are not, go back to the old win-lose style of negotiating. If you can reach a two-way exchange of information, you will find that you can create more total value in the transaction. The result is a structure to the sale that gives the items to one party that they value most, while giving the items to the other party that they value even more.

Listen

Be sure to listen actively, without being distracted by trying to present your point of view, as you can do that after you understand the other person's point of view. Let them talk, do not interrupt, and express some empathy for their position, as it shows them you can connect with their feelings. In other words, show you can relate to their feelings, even though you may disagree with their position. But, do not be too empathetic; striking a balance between empathy for the others and asserting your needs makes the difference between reaching a deal smoothly or having the emotions escalate as negotiations fall apart. A good way to strike this balance is to present your position as an additional feature of the transaction, not as a confrontational challenge to their position.

Ed Brodow, in *Negotiation Boot Camp*, suggests the 70/30 rule: He says to listen 70 percent of the time and speak 30 percent of the time. I think this is an excellent target to aim for. I say that knowing that I talk more than 30 percent of the time, but when I aim to talk only 30 percent of the time, I listen much more. Always listen more than you talk, as better negotiating is about better listening, not better talking.

Develop trust

In *Trump Style Negotiations*, George Ross indicates that you have to establish trust and a friendly relationship as a part of the negotiating process and as a crucial element to a successful result. This is hard to do with some agents. My beginning point is to find something in common. With all my years, all my family, and all my experiences, I can find some common ground with anyone by discussing families, sports, occupations, recreation, hobbies, reading interests, childhood, travels, heroes, villains, memories, or hopes.

Respect and listening develop trust. The only people you trust are the ones who care about you. Show that you care by listening. Then, show respect for your counterpart by asking what is important to them, and listen some more. You know how badly you feel when someone does not listen to you, so no listening means no trust. Besides, listening is sometimes the entire solution to the problem, as many people are just looking for someone to listen to their concerns.

Test the trust by revealing something about your client's interest. If you get something in return, it is working. If not, you might have to go to win-lose mode.

Issues not emotions

If your counterpart attacks, you do not have to—nor want to—have the primitive reactions of a counter-attack or becoming defensive. Instead of mimicking their rude behavior, set an example of cooperative behavior and lead them into a collaborative mode. If you act like an adversary, so will they. If you act like a partner, some agents will follow your lead. This is easier said than done, as it can be so emotionally tempting to fight back. You can only directly control your own emotions, but by presenting a positive role model you may be able to influence your counterpart to avoid hostilities.

In *Bullies, Tyrants and Impossible People*, Ronald Shapiro and Mark Jankowski describe their own version of collaborative negotiating, using the acronym NICE. The N stands for "Neutralize emotions," so that you can concentrate on the issues—that is, you act instead of react. They describe how you manage the normal human reaction of fight or flight by controlling your emotions through focus. You get so focused on nothing but the issues that you do not engage in battle. To neutralize your emotions, they suggest changing your physiology, with examples of breathing, taking a break and putting a finger over your lips to remind yourself to think before you speak. They also suggest changing your psychology, by replacing limiting beliefs that hold you back with empowering beliefs that improve your confidence. They use the wonderful term "miniphobias" to refer to limiting beliefs. In other words, turn off the messages in your head of self-doubt and replace them with messages of self-confidence. Greater confidence creates a presence that exudes more negotiating power, which makes your point of view seem more credible.

If you can understand why your counterparts are behaving in a difficult manner, and understand the relative values of their needs and wants, you can more easily control your own behavior. First, look at the situation from their perspective, so you can understand their motivation. Then, try to get them to put themselves "in your shoes" so they can see it from your side. With mutual appreciation, it is easier to eliminate hostilities, particularly if the appreciation leads to respect. So keep your focus on the issues instead of the emotions.

One of the byproducts of eliminating confrontational emotions is it reduces the anxiety and stress in the negotiations. The result is a happier experience for everyone, which leads to repeat and referral business. Since the other real estate agents are also your repeat customers, you want them to feel glad when they get to come back and sell another property with you.

Get the deal together

Once you know your needs and your counterpart's needs, you can see where they meet and where they diverge. The agreements are easy. The disagreements are where you earn your money.

If both sides participate in the brainstorming of the issues in the sale, they get a "pride of authorship" that makes the sale come together and stay together. This is why asking your counterpart for proposed solutions is valuable, as everyone appreciates being asked for their advice. If they suggest the way to resolve the difference of opinion, you know they will support their own idea. If you cannot get them to suggest a solution, float your own proposal. "What if the buyers do not ask for the washer, dryer, and refrigerator;

will the sellers have an easier time paying the closing costs?"
(Asking for your counterpart's advice shows respect for their
opinion, and gets them working with you.)

One of the most important components of collaborative
negotiating is exploring options. Just engaging in the process
of finding options creates cooperation. If you present a series
of options, your counterpart has choices, and that can get
you past an impasse. Since they get to choose, they feel in
control and that they've won something. Be careful, however,
that you do not give the impression that you will accept any
of the choices if you are just throwing them on the table for
discussion, as you may end up with an upset counterpart
who feels you are backing down from a commitment. Some
techniques for creating more options are to ask your counterpart what they would do if they were in your position, ask
what would happen if (insert name of sticking point) were not
a problem, and ask what would be wrong with a proposed solution. The first technique gets the counterpart to look at the
issue through your eyes. The second focuses directly on the
issue to see the consequences of eliminating that problem.
Since most people love to criticize, the third technique is
disarming as it asks for criticism.

The extra time involved in working together makes it
more likely that a deal will be reached, as neither party will
want to waste the effort involved in getting the negotiations
to this point. Also, getting agreements on the easy issues
leads to a pattern of working together, which makes the
tougher issues more likely to be resolved. So, start with the
easy issues first and gain some momentum. If you get really
stuck, go back to the beginning to review all your successes
so far, then see if you can get the final points done.

To get some support for a compromise, use examples of
what other people have done in the same situation. Lawyers
use precedents to help guide decisions, as they look at what
other judges decided when faced with the same situation.
Real estate agents can do the same. For example, if you are

negotiating with a builder who is resistant to paying certain closing costs for the buyer, show the builder all the other builders who offer to pay those closing costs and it will make it easier for the builder to follow that common practice. You can also bring in an expert to guide a decision. So, if the home inspector is raising issues about the foundation where the buyer and seller disagree, bring in a civil engineer to guide the resolution.

Do not confuse kindness with weakness. You are being considerate, but you are also asserting your client's most important interests and winning the most important points that are essential to your client. The proper assertion of your client's interest is more important than any personal bonding with another agent.

Learning how to negotiate in a collaborative manner will produce more sales, sales that close more easily, and more satisfied customers on both sides of the sale. You have to listen to your counterparts, understand what is important to them, and create the exchange of real interests. Instead of thinking about how to divide up the pie, work on making the pie bigger, so there is more for each side. Not only will the decreased anxiety that comes from this style of negotiating be good for your business, bringing agents and customers back again and again, but you might live longer with less stress.

Now that you know the types of negotiating, and how to use each one, you need to know the importance of knowledge and preparation because the more you know the better your results will be.

Chapter 4

Knowledge is Power

"Knowledge is power." This phrase, coined centuries ago by Sir Francis Bacon, presents one of the most important concepts in negotiating. For example, your client wants to buy this cute house, and the price seems good. Let's say you know that the seller has received a notice from the mortgage lender beginning the foreclosure process; would that affect your offer? Isn't that one of the easiest questions in this book? That is why knowledge is power.

Internet is Knowledge

We are in the Internet age. This means you have a golden opportunity to find out a lot about the property and the person before you start negotiating. Google is a great tool, but so are MySpace, Facebook, LinkedIn, Twitter, Active Rain, Diggit, BlogSpot, Friendster, Bebo, VillageMaker, and other social networking sites. Find out if anyone involved in your negotiations has a blog, as you can get a feel for what is important to them by reading their entries. If you are dealing with younger people, look at YouTube to see if they have posted any videos.

I had an offer on a property in California, and I wanted to know more about the buyer, so I Googled his name. When I found out that preservation of open space was important to him, I emphasized how the house he was interested in purchasing was surrounded by a nature preserve that is bigger than Central Park in New York. This greatly improved the quality of this buyer's offers.

To learn about the property, look to the Internet for sources and public records. In most states, the tax records will tell you when the property was purchased and for what amount. If you know your way around the Web, you can look up the loans on the property; the covenants, conditions, and restrictions; as well as possible liens.

Residential Property Disclosure is Knowledge

In North Carolina, you typically get the Residential Property Disclosure statement before you make an offer. In California, you get it after a contract is negotiated. The California system favors the seller, as the buyer does not know about the defects in time to add them to the negotiations over the price. Keep in mind that the amount of information available, and the timing of the delivery of that information, varies from state to state. Use every bit of information you can to help your proposal succeed.

Chatting for Knowledge

There is an even better substitute for the required disclosure: talk. The stereotype is that women like to talk. Most of them do. You will be surprised how much men also like to talk. In fact, real estate agents everywhere tend to be chatty. So, call the real estate agent for the seller or buyer and talk. Start with something personal about the real estate agent or yourself, just to be cordial. Then, once you are telling each other friendly stories, go on to the property and the client. If you are good at this exchange, you can give the other party only what you want them to know, and they will feel like they have inside information. If you are not, you will find that everything you have said "can and will be used against you," unless you have a collaborative negotiation where both sides are sharing information that is useful in putting a deal together.

So how can you get your counterpart to share information with you? One way is to ask for help. For example, you receive an offer on your listing that is way too low. You ask the buyer's agent to help you to come up with "ammunition" to present the offer better to your client, asking what they used to determine the price. Most agents will tell you everything they have to support their position, giving you the opportunity to prepare to counter those points when you present your counter offer. You can embellish this process by playing a little coy and asking them to help you understand their points, so that you get to probe deeper into any reasoning they may have. An option is to ask how the buyer's agent would present this offer "if you were in my shoes," although this phrase normally gets a more defensive reaction out of the other agent.

Know What Your Counterpart Knows

What you know can be used to help you. Also, what you know that the other party knows can be used to help you. In other words, if you know that the other party has certain information, you can use that knowledge to your benefit.

I was selling my own home in Rancho Palos Verdes, California, in 1995. We were negotiating with buyers, represented by a rookie agent, who made offers with strange conditions. Another set of potential buyers came through our house. My wife, Judy, happened to be home and overheard the lady of this new couple tell their real estate agent, "This house is perfect. We've got to get it." This statement is the reason why you coach your clients to be careful what they say around the seller. This new buyer made a good offer. If my wife had not told me this story, I might have just accepted it, as it would have been a joy to be rid of the other potential buyer.

However, I knew the new buyers had to get this house, so what I knew helped me. Also, I knew that they were aware that I had another offer that we were negotiating. So, what I knew that they knew helped me. We made a full price counter offer and agreed to some of the non-price terms in their offer so that they could win on some points in the negotiations. The new buyers signed it immediately. The sale was wonderful with people who really appreciated the property

When you have more than one offer, you need to reward anyone who brings you an offer by giving all the agents every opportunity to get the deal. I did that with this rookie agent by telling her I had another offer and that she would need to make another proposal quickly, since the time limit on my last counter offer to her clients had expired. When the rookie did not respond in time, I was happy to work with the good buyers—and happy to be free of the other buyers.

The Image of Knowledge Is Power

Margaret Thatcher explained the perception of power perfectly when she said "Being powerful is like being a lady. If you have to tell people you are, you aren't." In real estate negotiating, the perception of knowledge and ability creates the image of power. A major part of this image comes from your own belief that your position is powerful. Nothing persuades people as effectively as your own conviction in what you are saying. Similarly, it is easy to exude confidence, and thus the appearance of power, if you actually have all the knowledge necessary to complete the deal.

Margaret Rome, a real estate agent in Baltimore, Maryland, was a pediatric emergency room nurse before becoming a real estate agent, so she knows how doctors work. She uses an analogy to a surgeon to explain how you need to develop as a negotiator. You can read all the medical books you want, but until you have practiced surgery, you are not an experienced surgeon. The ability to have the "touch" to carefully handle delicate situations is developed by practice in both surgery and negotiations. Crisis management is an essential skill in the emergency room, a talent that rookies normally do not have. Just as you trust an experienced surgeon, you can feel a sense of trust in an experienced negotiator, as the confidence comes through.

Before the emergency room doctor takes charge, the unknown fuels your fear. When the emergency room doctor explains what is going to happen, even if it is not good news, there is a sense of relief as you find out what is wrong and what will be done to deal with it. Similarly, a good negotiator can create a similar sense of well-being by explaining what is going on, what the next steps will be, what the probable results will be, and what the ultimate result will likely be. Just as doctors do not promise excellent results, a negotiator can only predict a range of outcomes and never promises perfection. If you know how to manage the crisis, that knowledge is the power that is most appreciated by clients.

Know the Market

It's important to know the market in general, and then the specifics of your particular part of the market. In *Trump Style Negotiations,* George Ross makes that point that knowing the citywide averages is nearly meaningless because you need to know the statistics for your specific neighborhood. For example, in 2008 in Cary, North Carolina, any property priced under $250,000 is in a strong seller's market i.e. a market that favors the seller because there are few homes for sale in that price range and they sell quickly. So, you'd better make an offer quickly, come in with good terms, and try to wrap up the contract before someone else comes along. If you are in the same city at the same time, but the house is priced over $600,000, it is a strong buyer's market. You may start lower, move up in smaller increments, and ask for more concessions like Home Warranties, seller paid closing costs, and possibly some allowance for redecorating. In other words, if you are in a raging seller's market, you will have a different game plan than if in a raging buyer's market, and you will need to have the knowledge of each segment of the market to know how to proceed in that segment.

To know the general market, you need to know the relative supply of homes for sale compared to the number of homes that are selling each month. If it will take more than six months of selling at the current rate to sell the present supply, it is a buyer's market. If it will take less than six months, it is a seller's market. You should know this information for all the homes in the total market, and for the homes like the subject property in its sub-area of the market. You need to know the normal time it takes to sell, as expressed in days on the market. You need to know how many permits are being taken out for new homes, so you can tell if the supply of housing will be increasing or decreasing compared to the current demand.

With the recent changes in financing, you need to know the financial characteristics of the area, particularly whether the job market is increasing or decreasing, and what kind of jobs are being created to know what price range of housing will be supported by those jobs. It is particularly important to know what loans are available, and the requirements for getting those loans, so that you will know how many buyers can actually close a sale.

In addition to knowing the market in general, you need to study the subdivisions and local area of the subject property. Is it prestigious, so that premium pricing is appropriate, or just delusional so that the prices will not hold? What are the schools like, and are they stable? What other amenities are nearby, like shopping, entertainment, and places of employment?

Then, you need to know the characteristics of the subject property, and determine whether those characteristics add or detract from the value in the eyes of the market. In *Secrets of Winning the Real Estate Negotiating Game*, Seth Weissman and Ned Blumenthal have a list of 30 items that should be considered. You will need to make your own list that applies to your area. For example, in Palos Verdes, California, a view is an extremely important component for a property's value. In Raleigh, North Carolina, a view is not as important, as you cannot see beyond the trees from the vast majority of the homes. As you can imagine, every area has different features that affect the values. What's important is that you can demonstrate your knowledge of the market and thus earn your client's trust.

Know the Media Image of the Market

Your client's well-meaning friends are the worst influence when you are trying to apply your knowledge of the market, as they have seen the news media and think they know it all. (My favorite examples of this are fathers of daughters, and I am one, so I know the type well. We fathers try to show how much we know, whether we have accurate sources of information or not.) Since the normal source of information for well-meaning friends is the media, you have to understand how it works.

The media only have time to give a sound bite of information, so they condense an idea into one phrase. For

2008, the phrase was "buyer's market" and the lead story was foreclosures, so they applied it to the entire United States. That notion makes about as much sense as one weather report for the whole nation—that is, giving the average or median weather for the entire United States. What would you think of a weather reporter who took the feed from the national NBC station and said, "The weather today across the entire country, is 42 degrees, partly cloudy, with a three-mile-an-hour breeze from the southeast" If you averaged all the data, that is what you would get. That report would be useless for Palos Verdes, California, where the temperature is 73, and the weather is sunny and calm; and equally inane for Burlington, Vermont, where it is 14 degrees, snowing, with a 30-mile-an-hour wind from the north.

All weather is extremely local, reported with high definition radar that can distinguish individual road intersections. All real estate is extremely local, but reported in short sound bites averaged for the entire nation. Yet well-meaning friends try to take these generalized sound bites and apply them to their local surroundings. It is not the media's fault; they provide information and entertainment. It is our fault as real estate agents to let the well-meaning friends have more influence on the buyers and sellers than we do.

I have many examples of well-meaning friends. We were negotiating on a five-unit apartment in San Pedro, California, in 2003. There were six offers already made on the property, as it was the beginning of the raging seller's market. Real estate agents saw it coming, but the media was not aware of it yet. Our buyer was concerned about the type of roof on the property and talked to his friend about it. His friend told him that the media were saying it was a buyer's market and convinced him to include a provision for the seller to replace the roof in our offer. We could not talk him out of it by explaining the type of market we were in. With six offers, the seller was not going to be bothered with replacing the roof, even if we'd offered above the asking price, as someone else was sure to be offering above the asking price without asking for anything. Since the client had not worked with us before, and trusted his friend who had bought several properties with other real estate agents, we had to put the term in since it is our obligation to present all offers.

We did, and it came right back with the word REJECTED written boldly across each page. We did not even get the counter offer that the other six offers received. The property more than doubled in value in the next three years and would have provided a positive cash flow for our buyer.

So, have the knowledge of the market, and do your best to let your client have the advantage of your knowledge. Knowledge is power, but you have to get your client to listen to you instead of the media or their well-meaning friends.

Know the Parties' Motivation and Issues

Knowing why the buyer wants to buy and the seller wants to sell, as well as any time pressures or other issues they are facing, make up some of the most important points of knowledge. Here are some of the questions to pose to the seller:

- Why are they selling?
- Are there issues like divorce that affect their decision?
- Is their time pressure to sell, and how soon do they need to close?
- How long has the property been on the market?

- Has the seller purchased another property or found another one they have to have?
- Is it a corporate relocation, and if so does the seller have any relocation benefits?
- Is the property being sold by an unrepresented seller (FSBO) or with a reduced commission?
- Did the property have a sales contract before, and if so what happened?

Ask other questions to get some indication of the seller's personality types, such as where they work, what kind of work they do, and are they involved in any charities or community organizations. When you go through the house, look at the photographs in the house, as they give an indication of personality type, which we will discuss later. Also look for other things that bring up questions that you should ask. For example, look for the signs of a divorce, some of which are:

- Less furniture than normal, particularly with dents in the rug where furniture used to be
- Clothes for only one sex in a closet, with some of the other closet space empty
- Space where pictures used to be
- Missing cooking tools in the kitchen

The seller may have some benefits that may be advantageous to your client. You have to know the inner workings of relocation benefits to take advantage of the seller's benefits. Not only do some companies pay the seller's commission, but some also provide a "buy out" that comes with a bonus if the company does not have to buy the property. For example, IBM used to have a program where the seller could sell for up to 3% below the buy out figure and the seller would get the buy out figure as well as a 2 percent bonus. So, your buyer will get a discount price 3 percent below market and the seller will get a much higher net figure. For example, the home has a "buy out" of $200,000 from IBM, so that if the owner does not sell it IBM will buy it for $200,000. If the seller sells it for anything above $194,000, the seller will receive the $200,000 buy out payment from IBM and a $4,000 bonus. Remember when you are making an offer that the seller also has the other choice to take the buy out offer, so there are limits on the range in which the seller will sell because the seller will not go below what can be obtained from the buy out. You have to find out not only which company the benefits are from, but which relocation package they have. Many listing agents do not know the benefit package, so you have to get them to ask.

Another saving that most real estate agents keep in mind in their offers is the savings on the commission by a non-represented seller (commonly called a For Sale By Owner, with the nickname FSBO). Since the seller is not paying a commission to a listing agent, most real estate agents reduce their offers by the amount of the commission.

Similarly, you need to know the motivation and issues of the buyer. My favorite way to ask for this information is "Tell me about your clients," with a smile. Some of the information you are trying to learn is:

- Where are they moving from?
- How soon do they need to move?
- Is this a corporate relocation, and do they have relocation benefits?
- Where do they work, and what do they do for a living?
- Do they have friends or family in the neighborhood, so they will stick with a purchase more than someone who is not attached to the neighborhood?
- How large is their family, do they have children, and if so what age(s) (so you can determine if schools are important)?

♠ Are there any features in a home, or the neighbor-hood, that are necessary for them to have?

If you are reviewing an offer, ask what terms can you include in the counter offer to make your counterpart look good, and find out the relative importance of the issues in the offer. For example, do the buyers need the seller to pay the buyer's closing costs? If paying the closing costs is absolutely essential, be sure to give a counter offer that has the seller paying the closing costs. If you give your counterpart some terms that make them look good, your counterpart becomes more active in selling their client.

The buyer's financial qualification is a line of questioning in itself. It is an area of investigation that every buyer's agent should pursue before deciding to work with a client. As a listing agent, I have never had an agent tell me that their buyer is not financially qualified, in all 29 years of practice. Yet I have had sales fail to close because the buyer could not get the financing. So I ask for a pre-approval letter, and I call the person who signed it. My favorite discussion was with a lender who said he did not recognize the name of the buyer. I faxed the pre-approval letter to him and called back. He said that was not his signature and he had never heard of that buyer. Needless to say, the offer did not go much further after that.

In *Trump Style Negotiation*, George Ross has a good ap-proach to this concept. He feels that there are three things you must learn about the other side: (1) constraints, (2) motivation, and (3) negotiating weaknesses. The constraints are anything that limits your counterpart's ability to make a deal. The motivation creates their enthusiasm for the deal, or lack thereof. The negotiating weaknesses are things to exploit, such as deadlines that will cause the counterpart to make concessions.

Pay attention to everything you see and hear about your counterpart, then develop questions to probe what you think you see and hear. You will never get an all-inclusive list of questions (and if you did, it would be so long the other agent would not answer them). After practice, you will get a sense of what is important, and will learn which are the key elements to focus on.

Know the Personality

Knowledge is not confined to the property; you must also know the people involved in the negotiations. One part of knowledge that is often overlooked is determining not only the personality type of the people you are dealing with but also of yourself. Analyzing a personality type means you look at a person's collection of habits that has been developed from what has worked for them in the past. Since the goal of successful negotiations is satisfaction for both sides, you have to realize that satisfaction is a subjective emotional state that is tied in with a person's personality. In other words, what would make one personality type happy might not please another.

Many professionals and psychologists have developed ways of grouping people into categories that helps predict their tendencies and behavior. There are a number of different examples in the Appendix, but I will focus here on the personality profile that works for me.

George Ross hits the nail on the head when he explains in *Trump Style Negotiation* that you adapt your style of communicating to the person you are negotiating with and to the circumstances of the negotiation. Intuitively, we all understand that you do not use the same style of discussion for a construction worker at a noisy jobsite that you would use for a meeting with a CEO and her husband at their luxury home. In other words, you want to follow the Platinum Rule of treating others the way they want to be treated. But, how do you profile the personalities in order to adjust your presentation?

Marston's DISC Personalities

The system that works for me is the DISC personality profiles, attributed to William Moulton Marston, as it is simple to understand and easy to spot the characteristics that put someone in one group or another. There is not room here to go into a comprehensive discussion, but a short review will give you the gist. In essence, Marston ranks people along two traits. The first is a scale that rates how open or supporting they are on one end and how guarded or controlling they are on the other end. The second is a scale that ranks how direct or indirect the person is. By having one scale run north/south and the other run east/west, the scales divide people into four groups. Howard Brinton has an extensive discussion of this personality profile available through www.GoStarPower.com. Here is a short summary of each group:

1. **D stands for Dominance**, people who are direct and controlling. This person is used to dealing with problems and challenges. Normal terms applied to someone with high scores on this personality trait are demanding, forceful, egocentric, strong willed, driving, determined, ambitious, aggressive, and pioneering. They want condensed information, and they make quick decisions.

2. **I stands for Influence or Inducement,** depending on which writer you read. This person is direct and supportive, likes to influence others, and tends to be emotional. Terms used to describe a high I person are convincing, magnetic, political, enthusiastic, persuasive, warm, demonstrative, trusting, and optimistic. They want to know who else bought houses like this, and typically have pictures of themselves with important people.

3. **S stands for Steadiness, or Submission**, again depending on your source. This person is indirect

and supportive. wants a steady pace and security, and does not like sudden change. Terms for a high S personality are calm, relaxed, patient, possessive, predictable, deliberate, stable, consistent, and unemotional. They are normally very family oriented so look for family pictures around their home or office.

4. **C is for Conscientiousness or Compliance,** if you want to use Marston's term. This person is indirect and controlling and adheres to rules, regulations, and structure. A C person likes to do quality work and wants to get it right the first time. Words used for a high C personality are careful, cautious, exacting, neat, systematic, diplomatic, accurate, and tactful. Visualize a CPA or the stereotype for an engineer, and you have an image of a C.

When you are looking for knowledge, look for what type of person you are negotiating with. Find out what kind of work they do, what hobbies they have, ask them about their family, and take a look at their office or their home. Check them out on a search engine like Google™, which may have several references to them.

Some general pointers:

- Do not bore a **D** with details or lots of forms to fill out. Give information in bullet points. Then let them feel like they're the one who cleared all the obstacles out of the way and that they put the deal together.
- Tell the **I** that all sorts of important people are doing what you want them to do, that the property is very popular and prestigious. Brand name builders are important to an **I**.
- If you are negotiating with an **S,** do not come up with any quick surprises, and emphasize the benefit of safety and security for their family.

⬧ If you are negotiating with a **C**, emphasize how your proposal follows the rules of procedure, and give them lots of data—a couple of charts, graphs, and an Excel spreadsheet would be wonderful.

The knowledge of someone's personality will affect your choice of a game plan as well as how you talk, present, and relate to them. If you are negotiating with a D, do not plan on a lot of offers and counter offers. Let the I think that someone else is going to come along and get the property. Keep your proposal to an S simple and safe. If you are negotiating with a C, put lots of detailed terms in the proposal and be ready for the decision to be studied to death.

Know how you think: Visual, Verbal, Kinesthetic

We have looked at personality profiles to analyze how people behave. Now, let's look at the way they process information, that is, how they think.

Some people are *visual*: they think in pictures. Some people are *verbal*: they think in words and stories. Some people are *kinesthetic*: they want to see how it feels and mull it over. An easy way to tell a visual person is that many of them talk fast. If someone speaks very quickly, they typically have to think in pictures, and their words have a hard time keeping up with all the images they can process. They also use visual expressions, such as, "How does that look to you?" Most American men are visual, that is why magazines aimed at men have mostly pictures, but there are plenty of American women who are visual. If you want to know if you are visual, close your eyes and think of a childhood memory, like the school you went to when you were 12. If you see a picture of the event, you are visual.

A verbal person will tell you stories. They like words and will string them together to create images. Most of them do not talk fast, and they use non-visual terms, such as, "How does that sound to you?" Most American women are verbal, although there are plenty of American men who are also. To determine if you are verbal, again think of a childhood event, and if you hear the sounds of that situation, you are verbal.

Kinesthetic people like to roll around in their thoughts before they finish them. They normally speak very slowly, and pause in the middle of the thought to fully enjoy every part of it. Since I am highly visual and normally want to get to the point, I have had to learn to let kinesthetic people take their time. When you close your eyes and remember a childhood event, if what you get is the feeling of that situation, you are kinesthetic.

How do you use this information?

If you know someone's personality type and whether they are visual, verbal or kinesthetic, you can relate to them on their own terms. Do not follow the Golden Rule; follow the Platinum Rule: Treat others the way they want to be treated, and relate to them on their own terms. If your counterparts are visual, talk and relate to them in visual terms—even send pictures with your emails. If they are verbal, tell the full story with all the embellishments. If they are kinesthetic, let them savor every moment of the discussion.

When you talk, present materials, and write documents based on your counterpart's personality and type. It is similar to speaking to someone in their native language. George Ross describes it as being a chameleon in *Trump Style Negotiations*—you adapt to your surroundings. While it is important to adapt to your counterpart, it is equally important to do it sincerely, as a fake performance loses all your credibility.

What if you do not know anything about their personality or type? Assume the real estate agent is a **D**, as most of them are, with a second choice of **S**. It is hard to miss a **C**, so you will not be guessing about them for long. Then, assume that men are visual and women are verbal, as most of them are. Start from there, and the response will normally give you a better idea of who you are dealing with.

If you know the personality types of the people in the negotiations, you can treat them in a manner that they will appreciate, which makes the deal go together more easily and close more smoothly.

> *I represented James and Lisa, sellers who owned a home in North Raleigh, North Carolina. When I talked to her over the phone, she had a list of detailed questions and had read every part of the contract. She told me long stories about what they wanted to do and why they were selling the house. So, I had a C personality who was verbal. James rarely entered into the discussions, but when he did it was right to the point, and he immediately fixed everything that needed to be improved to market the house. He was a D personality who was visual. We sold the property to a single woman whose Internet information indicated she was very career oriented and worked in an engineering position; I guessed she was a C. Her agent had a website that talked all about herself but looked homemade and did not have much detail, only the main points. I guessed she was an S, as the website talked a great deal about stability and continuity.*
>
> *The house we were selling was immaculate, typical for a C and a D. The buyer loved that aspect of it, as she would not have to deal with a comprehensive list of things she would want to do, something that appeals to a C. She made an offer that was fairly good, but we could not put it together when my D seller lost interest after it went back and forth on too many little points. I thought my sellers should come down and accept*

the offer, as the comparable values supported it. But the C seller pointed out all the details that were positive aspects to her house, something an appraiser does not consider in the appraisal report. The buyer walked away, briefly.

The buyer came back when she heard we were getting another offer. Isn't the fear of loss wonderful? My sellers were a little more reasonable after the costs of not selling the home got the selling C's attention. The buyer's agent and I discussed what I could put in my proposals that would make her client happy and what she could put in her offer that would make my clients more receptive. The offer provided for a quick closing, which made my D seller happy, and it had details about inspections and repairs that made the C buyer happy. In other words, knowing the personality types let us put provisions in the offer that would please each side.

The sale had its interesting points. The C buyer had a detailed list of things to be fixed. High D seller to the rescue, he jumped in and fixed many of the items himself, while getting receipts for everything he did. Our Team prepared a detailed analysis of all the repairs, with receipts attached, and made sure the buyer could walk through well in advance of the closing. The C buyer was happy with the detailed information that followed the rules of procedure.

Preparation is Power

One of the most important ideas to understand about negotiating is that it is not just an event; it is a process that starts well before the event. The Kentucky Derby may only last for two minutes, but there is a great deal of preparation that goes on before the horses come out of the starting gate.

PAIDS

Ron Shapiro and Mark Jankowski give a formula for negotiating in *The Power of Nice*. They call it the three Ps, Prepare, Probe, and Propose. Their preparation is similar to the discussion above where gaining knowledge creates power. Probing is a good way to start interacting with your counterpart, to find out their needs by asking them. As we discuss in collaborative negotiating, proposing solutions together leads to better agreements. However, the preparation part of the process is so important that Ron Shapiro and Gregory Jordan have written an entire book about it in *Dare to Prepare: How to Win Before You Begin*. They use an acronym called PAIDS:

- Precedents—how did others resolve the same problem, e.g., what did similar houses sell for?
- Alternatives—find more than one way to put the deal together.
- Interests—know what they really want.
- Deadlines—know what time pressure is pushing on any party.
- Strengths (and weaknesses)—what are yours, and what are your counterpart's? The answers will tell you how to work them to your advantage.

Once you have those items identified, the final two steps are (1) to determine your highest goal and your walk-away position, so you can aim high but be willing to end the negotiations when you are not getting what you need; and (2) develop a strategy (we will spend a chapter on developing a game plan).

The Harvard Way

Harvard Business School Publishing has a nine-step preparation to negotiations in its ManageMentor online service that is also discussed in *Negotiation* by Harvard

Business Essentials. In the Appendix, I have adapted their steps to specifically apply them to a real estate transaction.

This preparation is particularly important if you get to have collaborative, or Win-win, negotiations. In this type of negotiation, each party's knowledge is powerful, and if you share knowledge you can make the outcome much better. So, you can enhance the power of the entire process by bringing more knowledge to the negotiations, then sharing it so that both parties come up with a deal that gives each side what they value most.

Now that you appreciate the value of knowledge and preparation, you need to understand the possible structures of the negotiating process and how to use them to your client's advantage.

CHAPTER 5

STRUCTURE OF NEGOTIATIONS

Before you forge ahead with a real estate negotiation, you have to understand how the process is structured. It is like a dance, where people from different backgrounds and cultures dance differently. You can try to select different structures for negotiating, and that choice will have an effect on the process, which will have an effect on the result. In most sales, you have to follow what is traditional for your local area, so you will need to learn the local etiquette. Once you understand the structure you are working with, you can tweak it to influence the outcome.

If you are old enough, you remember the Vietnam War and how the negotiations in Paris were delayed because the participants argued over the shape of the table. Some wanted the table to be round, others wanted it to be square, and there was disagreement about which parties would be seated at the table. The structure of the negotiations was so important that these arguments went on and on, while people died in combat. What does this show? If the structure of a negotiation is so important that it's worth prolonging a war to settle it, you need to pay attention to the structure of your negotiations.

Three primary structures are used in real estate negotiations: the round table, the formal, and the informal. In the round table style, you get all the parties together, sit at one table, discuss the issues, resolve them, and come to a conclusion to either sign an agreement or determine that there is no deal, all before you leave the table. In the formal style, you have formal written offers, formal written counter offers, and a formal agreement that is a series of documents. The informal style starts with a formal written offer, is responded to with informal verbal counter offers, and finishes with the preparation of a final signed agreement. There are many other choices, but you can learn what you need to know from these three examples, then adapt them to any structure that is required in your area.

Round Table Negotiating

My favorite structure is to get all the parties together and directly identify the issues. You focus on where there is agreement, identify the disagreements, focus on those, and either come to an agreement or leave without a sale. The process is more honest, requires the parties to work together, and gets to a resolution more quickly. An example of a round table discussion is the best way to understand the process.

> *In the 1980s, my family developed a 37.5 acre oceanfront parcel on the California coastline. We started the development in a partnership with the Berry family and proceeded to get the first permit for development in Rancho Palos Verdes in the Coastal Zone that was controlled by the California Coastal Commission. The development had the last 17 lots that would extend right to the water on the Palos Verdes Peninsula. Oceanfront property is extremely valuable. For example, my old home in that subdivision is now for sale for $7,800,000.*

The twenty-five lot subdivision had been approved and we were ready to record the final tract map. Regulatory approval of a subdivision in the Coastal Zone took many public hearings as well as huge quantities of engineering, mapping, and Environmental Impact Reports, not to mention lots of money.

The Berrys were sophisticated partners. They knew that the tax rate for capital gains taxes was going to increase at the end of 1986 and that if they sold their interest in the partnership before the end of 1986, the capital gains rates would be lower. If they stayed in the development and participated in the sale of each lot, they would be considered dealers in real estate, and the gain would be taxed at the much higher rate for ordinary income. So, they wanted to be bought out of the partnership, and the transaction had to close before 5 p.m. on December 31, 1986, a deadline established by the Internal Revenue Code that could not be extended.

I sought out partners, and found Larry Schmidt of Watt Industries early in December. At the time, Watt Industries was one of the largest builders in California. After the due diligence review by Watt Industries, there were only two days left to put the deal together.

Ray Watt, president and founder of Watt Industries had all the parties meet at his office in Santa Monica the morning of December 3 for a round table negotiation. Everyone presented their positions, and we focused on the items of agreement. The Berrys were firm on their price, and Mr. Watt found it to be reasonable. Everyone started with a list of terms, and the items we agreed on were merged into one list. We discussed a revision to the partnership agreement for the Berrys to be bought out and my family to remain in the partnership. The attorneys for Watt Industries drafted a new partnership agreement early in the afternoon, some changes were reviewed, and a revised document was to be drawn up to be ready for the morning.

The draft of the proposed agreement said that the entire property would be subject to huge financing to allow Watt Industries to pay for the acquisition of the Berry interest and to pay for the improvements. If my family allowed that, it might end up that we would get nothing out of all of the effort. That evening, my mother, Lorna, suggested we should ask that our family got two lots free and clear of any financing, so that no matter what happened, we would at least have that. Indeed, the rest of the family thought there was no way Watt would go for the proposal, but decided to ask for it anyway, as backing down from an extreme request can be taken as a concession and might get us something of value.

The next morning, everyone gathered again at Watt's office. When we made our proposal, Watt countered that if we got two lots free of any financing, then they got two lots free of any financing, so that each of the partners received equal value. This example is a classic Win-win trade, as the value to our small organization of lots that were free and clear of any financing was much higher than the value to huge Watt Industries, who could finance anything. In other words, the value to us of having lots we owned outright was much more important to us, as we could then finance the lots to build our own homes. This offer meant that my brother would get one home and I another, both right on the ocean.

You never accept an offer too quickly, as the other party will think they should have offered less.

My family left the room to discuss the proposal and to make it look like it was difficult for us to accept, in order ot make the Watt organization believe they were driving a hard bargain. Out in the hall, we made sure to stifle our jumping for joy, then re-entered the room to indicate we were reluctantly accepting their proposal. The deal was finalized, a cashier's check was given to the Berrys for their payment, and we drove to the title company to finalize the insurance and record the documents. I still remember the attorney driving on a motorcycle between the traffic on the freeway, flying to the recorder's office to get the documents recorded.

The deal was finished with 38 minutes to spare—a representative from the title company stood in line at the recorder's office and the attorney dashed in just before it closed. If we had not structured the negotiations to use the round table style the homes in Lunada Pointe along Marguerite Drive (named for Marguerite Berry) and Laurel Drive (named for our daughter, Laurie) would not exist, and my family would not have grown up at 57 Marguerite Drive.

So, be sure to select the structure for the negotiations to have a chance to reach your goal in the time allowed. Also, facing each other and working together to reach an agreement on a personal basis was a great beginning to a wonderful partnership. I am still thankful to Larry Schmidt as he set up the round table discussion, worked hard to reach agreement, then supervised the construction of the entire project to be one of the most successful that Watt Industries ever had.

The Normal Real Estate Negotiating Structure

In real estate, negotiations around a table are unusual. Most of the negotiations are conducted either in the formal method of California or the informal method of North Carolina, so we will walk through those examples. You will need to know the local variations in your area, such as the way the final real estate contracts are drawn up by attorneys in different states.

Formal negotiations

In the formal method of California, real estate agents write up a formal offer and usually present it to the seller's agent. Some buyer's agents will insist on presenting the offer personally to the seller, with the agent present, with the goal of getting the seller to sign the offer before the end of the meeting. That rarely happens, as most sellers do not accept the first offer. However, the face to face meeting gives a negotiator a better opportunity to gather information and make a more effective presentation.

After the first offer is presented, the seller can accept the offer, reject the offer, or usually give a counter offer. The counter offer is given in a formal manner, in writing, specifying all of the terms that are not accepted. This written counter offer is presented to the buyer's agent, who presents it to the buyer. Once again, the choices to respond are to accept it, reject it, or give another counter offer. The amount of time to consider an offer or counter offer is normally three days, but can be shortened by the party making the proposal.

This process goes on until someone accepts a counter offer, or until no agreement is reached. To create a binding contract, one party signs the last counter offer, returns it to the other party, and gets a receipt that the other party received it within the time allowed. The final contract is the original offer plus all of the counter offers, so establishing the entire agreement requires going through the entire sequence and mentally crossing out all the terms that have been countered. The process lasts sometimes for weeks, with formal documents going back and forth. For example, my longest California negotiation had twelve counter offers.

Informal negotiations

In contrast, North Carolina uses informal negotiations, in true southern style. The beginning is the same with a written offer, but, it is usually presented only to the seller's agent. While the National Association of REALTORS® Code of Ethics provides the buyer's agent can present the offer personally to the seller, unless the seller has requested otherwise in writing, most listing agents in North Carolina would be upset if you did that. (It is not good to antagonize the seller's agent, as they have great influence on the seller, so you have to consider whether the advantage of personal presentation is outweighed by the disadvantage of antagonizing the seller's agent.)

The seller considers the offer, with the same choices of accepting, rejecting, or countering. Normally, there is a counter, which is discussed verbally and presented verbally to the buyer's agent, who discusses the counter with the buyer. They respond by accepting, rejecting, or countering. Any counter is also verbal, and typically presented in an hour or two from receiving the response from the seller. The seller and seller's agent discuss the response, and this verbal back and forth goes on until there is a meeting of the minds or a termination of negotiations. If there is an agreement, the buyer and buyer's agent modify the document by crossing out the terms that have been changed, initial the changes, and present it to the seller's agent. The seller's agent presents it to the seller. Once the seller signs and initials it and the acceptance is communicated to the buyer, there is a contract, which is easy to determine as it is all in one document. The process takes a few hours, occasionally a day or two.

Analyzing the systems

Compare this process of offers and counter offers in the traditional structure of real estate negotiations to round table negotiations. In the traditional structure, you take an opening position and defend that position with lots of reasons why it is fair, just, and correct. Then, when you respond to a counter offer, you abandon the position that you once defended, take another position, and give even more reasons for defending the new position. By taking the new position, it is clear that the old position was not the fair, just, and correct position that you represented. So you just undermined your credibility for the next round of negotiations.

Reaching an agreement in the traditional method of offers and counter offers requires ignoring the fact that both of you were posturing by presenting a series of illusions to come to the conclusion. In *Trump Style Negotiations*, George Ross explains that you have to learn that posturing, i.e. the face you put on for the negotiating process, does not necessarily reflect your reality. This process is not the finest way to create mutual trust. But the vast majority of real estate sales are negotiated in this manner. Even though this structure to real estate negotiating reaches an agreement after showing that each party was playing games when it defended the positions that it abandoned, and that each party is of dubious veracity, it then forces these parties who know they should not trust each other to work together to a closing. When my grandmother cooked squash for me as a six year old, she explained that I could "learn to like it" because I was not going to get out of eating it. So, you need to "learn to like" the traditional structure of real estate negotiating in your area, because you are not going to change it any time soon.

How to Use Structure to Your Advantage

So, learn the rules of the local version of the real estate game, and see how you can use them to your advantage. For example, the California version allows you to try to get a deal in one shot when you meet with the seller. Here is how you make a one shot presentation.

> *There was a five-acre parcel of vacant land on Marguerite Drive in Rancho Palos Verdes, California, that was a beautiful point jutting out into the ocean. The sellers were a group of private investors who had just foreclosed on the property, and there were several buyers interested. The sellers did not want the property; they wanted their money back and certainty of closing was important, the sooner the better. I represented a strong buyer, who also wanted the property, but at a discount price. If I used the normal structure of presenting a written offer and letting the seller consider it for three days, other offers would come in and my client would lose, as he would not come up to a competitive price.*
>
> *So, I got every financial qualification imaginable and wrote the offer with great terms such as a quick closing, short times for the buyer to review the geology, zoning, and title reports, and an offer with no financial contingency because the buyer was assured of getting the financing. Since vacant land can be hard to finance, having no financing contingency signaled the sellers that the buyer was confident of closing, so long as the property was not unbuildable.*
>
> *I scheduled a meeting with the sellers before anyone else was able to present an offer, and let the sellers verify the financial strength of the buyer before the meeting. I had reviewed the foreclosure*

information, and the offer was just enough for the seller to get their money back, but not anything more. In other words, I made sure my client offered at least the minimum amount I knew they would consider. At the meeting, I emphasized that the offer was "clean" and carried with it a large earnest money deposit. However, the offer expired if I left the office without their signature. I had to get it signed before anyone else had a chance to get to the property if I was going to get the price my buyer would accept. Losing a sure sale that achieved their goal was not worth the chance that a higher offer would come along, so the seller signed it.

Compare these structures of the negotiating processes, and you can learn to create an advantage for your client. If you are working in a state that has formal counter offers, shorten the time for the other party to respond if you are worried about competing offers coming in. You do not have to do that in North Carolina and the less formal states, as the offers are presented immediately and the responses are within hours. But, if you are in an informal state and find a real estate agent who is trying to wait for other offers, tell them your offer will be withdrawn unless you have a response within a short time.

One disadvantage to all the time allowed in the formal process is that the parties can "cool off" and lose interest. So if you are interested, respond in less than the allowed time to keep them warm. Don't respond so quickly, however, that you look too eager and lose your negotiating power.

The example illustrates how negotiating is an art, and how timing your response without signaling that you are too eager is learned by practice. The normal response time is three days, I usually respond within a day and a half to two days if I want to move the sale along. If I am hoping for other offers, I respond five minutes before the deadline.

You should figure out the features of the available structures to use them to your advantage. Similarly, you can always try to switch to a round table negotiation to completely change the process if you are good at meetings. If not, tweak the traditional structure to improve the chances of getting the results you need.

Now that you understand the structures of real estate negotiating, you need to learn how to develop a game plan to take your clients through the process to get to the results they want.

CHAPTER 6

GAME PLAN

Many people think negotiations start when the first offer is signed and end when it is accepted. It actually starts at the first point of contact with the client, and does not end with the closing of the sale. In most sales, there are at least two major points of negotiating: the first stage when you get a ratified contract and the second stage when you resolve any repair issues. With real estate sales becoming more international, however, you may deal with people from certain cultures who look at the signing of a contract as a statement of what they feel at that particular moment, and who, if the facts and feelings change, may want to change the contract. In that case, be prepared for many rounds of negotiations. As an example of negotiations extending after the closing of the sale, I have had buyers call after the closing wanting to continue negotiations on the condition of the house. My favorite one of these calls was from a buyer who wanted my seller to be responsible for the opossum that got into the house and ate the wiring on the dishwasher while they were remodeling a month after the closing.

The unknown is scary. Most people do not know the entire process of buying and selling real estate. So walk your client through all the steps in the negotiation, tell them what to do and what not to do, and answer all their questions. For example, coach your buyer clients that if they meet the seller or listing agent, they should not tell them that "they just have to buy this house," or "that it is the only one for them." Once your clients know the entire process, it will be less scary.

Before you start, figure out where you need to end up. First, figure out where you are, then where you want to be. Do not just figure out one ending point; look at the range of acceptable results. Look at what would happen if you were to aim high and focus on the best outcome you can imagine. Next, look at a mid-range result that you would be satisfied with and make that your primary target. Then, figure out your walk-away result, the one that is just barely acceptable and only slightly better than walking away. Figure out also your other choices, such as other homes for your buyer to purchase that would satisfy their needs, or other buyers who could purchase your property.

The party with the most alternatives in the negotiations has the most power. So figure out several ways to get from where you are to where you want to be. For each alternate route, evaluate what the various tactics would be, and decide how well you can predict the other party's response to each of those steps. Some choices may be easier for the other party to react to and thus increase your ability to predict their response. The more predictable path may have an advantage. Then, put all of the tactics together into a comprehensive strategy that becomes your game plan. As a part of this strategy, make a list of concessions that you are willing to make and ones that will never be made. This will help you decide what to concede first. It also helps to have a list of minor concessions so that you have something to throw in to give your counterpart one last victory to put the deal together. In short, visualize most of your moves before you begin.

For example, you want to buy a house for $425,000, when its asking price is $499,000. One strategy is to start with an offer of $399,000, hope the seller gives you a counter offer, and gradually work your way up to $425,000. It is hard to predict whether the seller will give you a counter offer, but it is easy to predict that the low-ball offer will upset the seller. Another choice would be to offer $425,000 as a "one shot" offer. This choice is less likely to upset the seller, but how predictable is it that the seller will not want to try you out with a counter offer, forcing you to walk away if you want to show it is really a one-shot offer? There are an infinite number of choices in between, particularly when you factor in the range of increases you might make in the counter offers, from small increases to large jumps. Another strategy would be to offer $499,000 fully furnished with both of the cars in the garage included. When the seller won't sell the furniture and the cars, drop the price to $425,000.

Needs vs. Wants

The most important part of your game plan is to separate what you need from what you want. The needs are absolute essentials, characteristics that are absolutely necessary to make a deal. In other words, if you do not get one of your needs, you will not make a deal. In contrast, wants are items you would like to have but could live without. As a further contrast, your stated position or posture is what you say you want, and it is frequently more than what you need. Then, you can start with everything you need and everything you want, and as you go through the negotiating process, give up the items that are wants and walk away if you have to give up one of your needs. The goal is to reach agreement, which is accomplished by satisfying the needs of the parties, not by satisfying their stated positions. So, concentrate on what is really essential to resolving the negotiations and try not to be sidetracked by the postures.

When you are taking a listing, an easy way to separate the wants from the needs is to ask the seller what items in the house are not negotiable; you will likely get a list of family heirlooms and items with high personal value. Then, shift to the other end of the spectrum and ask what items can be given away. You might find the sellers hate the washing machine and would rather leave it with the property. Then, you can fill in the hierarchy in between these two extremes by asking what else is important and what else is unimportant to them. As a part of discovering what factors about the house will come up in the negotiations, you need to find out what is wrong with it, as no house is perfect. You will rarely get a straight answer to "What is wrong with the house?" as most sellers are trying to sell you on how wonderful a product they have. Instead, ask "What improvements were you planning on doing if you had decided to keep the house?" They will give you a list of all of the flaws that you will have to deal with in the negotiations.

Expectations

You have to establish reasonable expectations. This process starts from the beginning of the relationship. Do not tell your buyer that you will find them the perfect house, because there is no such thing. Do not get your seller to think that you can get an impossibly high price. As you move into the negotiating stage, set up your game plan to aim at an achievable goal. If the buyer goes into the process expecting a ridiculously low price, your odds of success are slight. If the seller thinks the result will be over the asking price, it will not happen unless you are in a market that has multiple offers regularly, or unless you set the asking price way too low. If you set expectations at a level that is hard to achieve, you will occasionally have happy clients. If you set the stage with reasonable expectations, you will exceed the expected result some of the time. If you set expectations at a level that is easy to achieve, and if you develop good negotiating skills, you will exceed the expected result most of the time so you will get clients for life who refer all their friends.

How to Work With Alternatives

It is critical that you examine your alternatives to a negotiated agreement. As you go through the negotiations, keep in mind your other choice. Your client may not have to buy this house because there are other choices. It is particularly powerful as a buyer if you are willing to walk away from the negotiations. If there are several houses that your buyer likes, start with the one they like best, but if you do not get what they want, be ready to move on to the next. One strategy is to let the seller's agent know that you are negotiating on two houses, so that they feel the pressure of your other choice. If you are about to walk away, let your counterpart know that you are ready to move on to your other choices, and flash your alternative before their eyes. Many real estate agents just walk away and do not use this power. In Chapter 7, we will discuss how to Walk Away Slowly, so the other party can reach out to you and make the deal work on terms that are favorable to you.

John and Debbie had been relocated by IBM many, many times. They were good at it. We looked at more homes in a day than most buyers could see in a week. They narrowed the choices to three that they liked the best. Since they had a limited amount of time in Raleigh, we wrote up three offers, one for each of the homes they liked, and set up a game plan for presenting the offers. I presented one offer on the home they liked the best, though they did not like the location; John was willing to drive further every day if his payments were low enough. The builder did not accept our offer and countered at full price, even though I explained that we would move on if the price was not good enough. So I moved on to the next property, and presented the offer that had been written before they left town. The second builder countered at a much lower price

hoping to keep us from moving on to the next prop-
erty. I discussed the counter with the couple, and
we countered that offer. When the builder would not
accept those terms, we moved on to the next home.
The seller countered close to our asking price, we
countered that offer, and the seller accepted. We
had a complete game plan for the entire process,
and Debbie wrote me a wonderful, handwritten,
thank-you note.

Additional Items

Another part of your game plan is to throw in, or hold
back, additional items in the offer. My father-in-law, Gene
Friess, was a magnificent negotiator, probably the smoothest
I have ever seen. (That might be one of the reasons why his
daughter and my wife, Judy, out-negotiated me in fourth
grade.) He taught me to start negotiations with extra things
that you are requesting so you will have items to give up.
Some negotiators call this a Red Herring or a Decoy. I just
think of it as loading up with disposable baggage. Include
the washer, dryer, and riding lawn mower in your first offer
so you can give it up later in the negotiations. If you are negotiating for the seller, start your response to negotiations
by holding back something so you will have it available to
add later. For example, do not offer a Home Warranty in
the information provided in the Multiple Listing Service.
During the negotiations you can add the Home Warranty
to the benefits that the buyer is getting as a justification
for a higher price. The buyer will see some value in the
Home Warranty that was earned through negotiations, but
will not perceive its value if originally offered as part of the
sale. A great phrase to use in this situation is "let me see
if I can get that for you" so that the buyer's agent appreciates your accomplishment if you are able to get the item they
want.

It is important to be negotiating a number of things other than the price. Find out what terms are important to the other side, then give them something they want in return for something that is important to you.

I sold a home in Wake Forest, North Carolina, for a price that was very favorable to the buyer because my sellers wanted two things: (1) the security of knowing that their home would be sold and closed long before the completion of construction on their new home, and (2) to avoid moving twice. We found buyers who were retiring and did not want to move for months, but who were a bit frugal on the price, as they wanted to start their retirement without spending too much of their reserves. So we matched up the needs and wants of each side. The buyer got a great price but had to close early and let the seller rent the home back for a reduced rental.

When one side gets the items that are the most valuable to them and the other side gets the items that are most valuable to them, you get a Win-win result, but only if you have all the additional items in play.

Win Gracefully

Some people act like a bull (others describe it as a shark), trying to push the other side into accepting their point of view. Unless there is a reason why the other party cannot walk away, this style is less successful than most. Others use more gentle persuasion. One of the most successful is used by southern women, letting the other person think that the result is their idea, and "bless your heart," isn't it wonderful that you thought of that.

James Nellis of the Nellis Group in Virginia tells a story about learning negotiations from his real estate agent mother, Vicki, early in his career. They were at a closing and James planned on behaving like a bull, going after the sellers on a repair issue. He was about to start when he felt his mother touch his leg in a manner that he recognized as a signal to hold off. She proceeded gracefully to allow the sellers to offer to do what the buyers were looking for, smiled and closed the sale.

An important principle of winning gracefully is you do not have to be right, you just need to get the deal done. In fact, it is occasionally beneficial to apologize for something that is not your fault. Your lawyer will hate it, but that is what lawyers are for. Take responsibility for whatever happens, let your counterpart feel victorious, and get the deal signed.

Permission To Do the Opposite

One of the best negotiating tactics is to give the other party permission to do the opposite of what you want them to do. After all, the more you push and argue to get your counterparts to accept your position, the more likely they are to resist. If you push, they push back. So if you want them to accept an offer, give them permission to reject it as one of the choices you present. It is disarming. The attitude you want to convey is that you are not forcing them to sell, and that in fact it is all right with you if they don't sell.

If you have a counterpart that is desperate, it may occasionally work to hammer the other side into doing only one thing, with no feeling that they have a choice. But, it frequently leaves them unhappy about the result and looking for revenge. Give them permission to do the opposite so they can decide that they are in control, as they are the ones deciding to proceed. That victory for themselves makes it more likely that they will give you your victory.

A good example of this is to tell an agent representing a buyer that they should take their time in deciding to make an offer on the property. Go into the high level of interest that you have in the home, but do not push them to a feeling of a false sense of urgency. To embellish the presentation, say that you will call them if one of the many people showing the house makes an offer and then mention that they would then be in a bidding war with the other offer. Just give them permission to take their time deciding that this is the right home for them, and they will create their own sense of urgency and make an offer before someone else does.

Use Time to Your Advantage

The pressure of time can have a tremendous effect on the outcome of negotiations. Herb Cohen tells a story in *You Can Negotiate Anything* about his first trip to Japan to negotiate a major contract. The Japanese played with him until he was up against his deadline to leave the country, knowing he had to have an agreement before he left. His description that the results were worse than Pearl Harbor is vivid, as he had to concede way too much to get the deal done before his deadline.

Intuitively, you know that there will be a major difference in the time pressure between sellers who have retired and want to sell to move closer to their grandchildren, and sellers who have just received a foreclosure notice. There are all sorts of time issues, from people who have bought another home and do not want to make double payments to people who want to move before the beginning of their kids' school year. You will have sellers who have a contingent offer on another property who want to sell before someone else makes an offer on "their home," as well as banks who have foreclosed on a property and want to sell to get this REO property off their books. Find out what the time pressure is, and use it as part of your game plan.

Pareto Principle

Vilfredo Pareto created the 80/20 rule known as the Pareto Principle, which says that 20 percent of what you do produces 80 percent of the results, and 80 percent of what you do produces 20 percent of the results. You will find that 80 percent of the success in negotiating happens in the last 20 percent of the time you have available. Create a game plan that allows for patience, so that if you cannot get the results early in the process, you can set them aside until the deadline is approaching. This technique is only possible when you know your counterpart's time line. If you bring up a repair issue well in advance of the closing date, the seller may refuse to do it, as they have not arranged their moving van and eliminated the contingencies on the home that they are purchasing. If you discover that a repair has not been done properly during the walk-through the day before closing, the seller is under much more pressure to get it taken care of so that their other closing will occur and they will be able to move.

> *Peaches (her nickname) was a Registered Nurse and we were selling her family's home in Cary. Her husband had already taken a job transfer and she was still working in Cary with the kids. I got a call from Peaches one Saturday night asking if she had to allow a showing by someone who called from the driveway. She had two children in the bathtub, and it was already dark. I called the buyer's agent, who told me her clients needed to find a house in Cary before their flight back home left tomorrow. I called Peaches to tell her that buyers with a close deadline are the ones we want. She got the kids out of the*

tub, the buyers looked at the house, and we had an offer within the hour. We gave the buyers a counter offer within minutes, as you move quickly when it is to your advantage and "strike while the iron is hot." The "hot" buyers accepted our counter offer, even though it was extremely favorable to the seller. However, the buyers got to leave town knowing that they would have a home when they completed their job transfer.

Time to Adapt and Accept

Sometimes it is better to move slowly and make your counterpart invest more time. The more time invested, the more likely it is you will get concessions, because the counterpart will want to make a deal and not waste all the time and effort already spent. By moving slowly, you can gradually steer your counterpart to the desired result.

Moving slowly also works better when you need to give your counterpart time to accept a distasteful fact. If the house is not going to sell anywhere near the asking price that the seller expects, and you have a less-than-wonderful offer from an investor buyer on the table, give the sellers time to adjust their expectations. It may take time for them to realize that the world does not care that they need to get more money out of the house in order to pay off their credit card debts or buy a more elegant house, as the market only cares about the actual value of the property that is for sale.

Leslie McDonnel is a real estate agent in Libertyville (North Chicago), Illinois. To give her sellers time to adjust to the low offers that are prevalent in the 2009 market, she scans the offer and emails it to her clients. Then, she calls with a message that she is going out on an appointment, and will talk to them later after they review the offer. By giving them time to adjust, she does not have to deal with an upset client at the moment she learns how low the offer is. Instead, she deals with someone who has had time to face the reality of a strong buyer's market.

The time you take to do something also sends signals to your counterpart. If you respond too quickly to an offer or counter offer, you may show that you are too eager. Perceiving the signal that you are highly motivated, the counterpart may give you a tougher response. And if you want to check on how your counterpart is proceeding with a response to your offer, have a better excuse for calling than "I wanted to see if you received it." Otherwise, your eagerness is showing. There are occasions, like the Peaches story above, where responding quickly is to your advantage. Knowing when to be quick and when to be slow is part of learning the art of negotiating.

Advantage of a Game Plan

One of the best parts of creating a game plan and discussing it with your client is that it reinforces the image that you completely understand the process and have it mastered. You discuss how you are going to start, then predict the range of responses. Typically, you will start with a reasonable proposal that asks for more than you need. When you get an expected response, the client will be properly impressed. Then, when you continue the game plan as predicted and get another predicted response, your value as a counselor will increase. Since you have planned the concessions you were going to make, your client will not see them as losses but rather as a part of the strategy. When you come to the predicted result, or better yet an improvement over the predicted result, you demonstrate negotiating mastery. However, be sure to forecast a range of responses, as no one can precisely predict the future or the response of a group of people.

Include as a part of your game plan a wrap-up discussion with your client just before closing. Go over all the things that worked out as you predicted, and show the value of having your services as a guide. It is important to leave the client with a last impression of how well the sale went.

I got a phone call from Charlie, a client whose family bought a home in Cary and moved in over Christmas. It was not the best time of the year to move, but he called to say how he enjoyed the process, because I had told him everything that would happen before it happened. Since I was able to guide him in that manner, he had complete confidence that the sale would work out and his family would be fine moving at a difficult time of year.

Now that you know how to plan out the negotiating process, you need to understand the principles to follow to create a great deal.

CHAPTER 7

PRINCIPLES OF REAL ESTATE NEGOTIATING

You need to develop certain principles that work for you in negotiating, then follow them nearly every time. Please notice the word "nearly," as I hardly do anything every single time. Negotiating is an art, with a little science that is mostly probability, so you need to know when to apply a principle—and when to shelve it. If you do not follow your standard principles, be aware of that decision and make sure you have a valid reason for changing from the standards that normally guide you to success. Violating a principle normally comes back to haunt you.

Here are some principles that work:

1. Your Client's Interests Are Paramount

Your client's interests come way in front of yours. Do not let your client miss buying the home of their dreams just because you want to do some fancy negotiating. If they think it is worth the price, be sure you give them your advice, but if they want to proceed, it is their life. When you are giving them advice that they do not follow, be sure to document it in writing. But, do not document it with something that sounds like a lawyer; do it with a style that sounds like you are writing to a relative asking them to reconsider.

In the same manner, if it is going to take forever to negotiate a deal on the property they love, your obligation is to take the time required to get the best deal. The best way to lose a client and all their referrals is to let them feel that you put your interest in making a quick deal in front of their interest in getting a good deal. So do not rush the process.

Another instance where your client's judgment is paramount is assessment of the success of the negotiations. You might think they went extremely well, but if the client is not happy, there goes your repeat and referral business. If you think you did not do well but the client is thrilled, your business will grow.

This is not to say that you always defer to your client's judgment. They are relying on you for professional counseling. If they want to overprice their home when they try to sell, it is not in their best interest, so you have to do everything you can to prevent it. In Chapter 8 you will learn Rule 12: Don't Let Your Clients Do Something Really Stupid.

The corollary to this principle is that you are negotiating your client's property, not your own. You advise; they decide. In this capacity, you should not take on the tone or position of the client when you talk to the other agent. By being a professional counselor, you can avoid emotional responses to the other agent when their offer is less than wonderful. Keep in mind that any offer is an opportunity to make a deal and must be presented. You do not have to be gleeful about it, but being insulting hurts the process.

2. Let the Other Side Feel that They Won

My mother, Lorna, enjoyed arguing and wanted to end the process feeling that she was right. It was a great education, because I learned very early that if I got the results that I wanted, it was not important for me to force the other person to feel that they lost. In fact, if I let my counterparts feel that they won, it was easier to get the results that I wanted, so they felt a "win" while I got a "Win".

Forcing your counterpart to recognize that you are victorious is counter-productive. If they feel that they won, they will do everything possible to close the sale smoothly. If they feel that they lost, they will do everything possible to have a victory before the sale closes.

This idea does not mean that you want your client to feel that they lost. Quite the opposite! You want your client to realize the great results they got in the final agreement. You just do not want to rub your counterpart's nose in the great results you got.

This concept is particularly useful when you are close to making a deal, and your counterpart fancies themself to be a great negotiator. Find something you can give them as a victory, no matter how small, so they can feel they won—especially if they need to show that victory to look good to a spouse. You do not need to be right; you need to get the deal done.

3. Don't Push; Present Choices

I have yet to meet anyone who says they like a pushy sales-person. We help people make decisions. I learned from Joe Stumpf of By Referral Only to act like a counselor when I am working with my clients. The best way to act like a counselor is to present the various choices to a client and discuss the advantages and disadvantages of each. Your clients know their life better than you ever will, so if they get complete, accurate information, they will make the right choice.

This principle is particularly appropriate for listing presentations. You discuss with the potential sellers that they can (1) decide not to sell, (2) go For Sale By Owner, (3) use a discount firm, or (4) use my Team. Present all the advantages and disadvantages of each choice, and if you are the right choice, they will come to it. The first advantage of this technique is that you get clients who really support the decision they made. The second advantage is that you avoid clients who are not right for you. There are some listings that you do not want.

Many people use the Ben Franklin Close: Mr. Franklin would divide a page into two columns, put the reasons in favor of one choice on one side and the reasons in favor of the other choice in the other. Then he would cross off items that were equal on each side of the line, and make a decision based on what was left. That method works well if properly set up with a commitment by the client to decide on what is left on the paper. But it only works for two choices and usually works best when you are deciding whether to do something or not. So I prefer the explaining a wider range of choices with the plusses and minuses of each choice.

4. Present with Confidence and Conviction

According to President Lyndon Johnson, "Nothing convinces like conviction." Everyone has had an agent present an offer saying, "I know it is low, but see if you can get us a counter offer." Don't do that. If you believe in your position, exude conviction.

In law school, they teach future lawyers that 10 percent of the effect is the words you say, and 90 percent is how you say it. Be confident in what you are presenting. Don't say this is your initial offer, that you want to run it up the flag pole, or that this offer is a good start. Each one of those phrases tells your counterpart that you are not serious about this offer. Present the offer as being a good offer.

Do not over-present the offer, however. Do not tell the other agent that you have a great offer for them when it stinks. You will lose credibility. However, you can always be glad that your client decided to make an offer on the property and can express that happiness. If you get a negative reaction from your counterpart, just deflect it by saying the people they should be upset with are all the other agents who have shown the property and not been good enough to bring an offer.

> *A true believer is much more persuasive than a hired gun. As an attorney, I helped a real estate agent friend who was falsely accused of an ethics violation involving displaying properties on the Internet. I have a conviction about the proper use of the Internet as a wonderful tool for real estate agents and consumers, so I am able to present that issue in a convincing manner. The hearing was going fairly well. I noticed a major reaction from the members of the panel when I told them I was not being paid for my work that day and that I had done all my research, driven for hours, and appeared at the hearing as a matter of protecting a principle that I believe in. My friend received the written ruling that the panel found in her favor the next day, which means they had to rule immediately for us with no reservations in order to have gotten the results in the mail so quickly. It was the right result, and may have occurred without my statement, but my conviction helped persuade the panel.*

5. Everything Must Be On the Table Before You Respond

Get all the terms on the table before you start negotiating. In other words, see the entire written offer so you can find out everything that the other side wants. Do not negotiate one item then have the other side bring up another item and negotiate that. If you do, you will be making concession after concession as the other side "nickel and dimes" you to death. Find out what all the terms and conditions are, then work with your client to identify the ones they can live with and isolate the ones that need adjustment. Since you have your game plan set up to get what is absolutely necessary, identify the wants you would like to have but could live without and then proceed.

When I had just started selling real estate in North Carolina, I had a listing for which the buyer was about to go out of town and my seller was desperate to get the home under contract because their family had to be relocated for business. The agent for the buyer was an extremely popular agent with my firm, Prudential Carolinas Realty, and she called to say there was not time to write the whole offer, get it negotiated, then revised and signed before her client left town. The agent was afraid that her indecisive buyer would make her look at dozens more houses if she did not get a deal on this house before the trip, because she would change her mind by the time she came back. This was in the 1990s, when technology did not let you send documents everywhere quickly. So I had the agent give me the terms of the offer over the phone, called my client, discussed it, got a counter offer, presented it, the buyer accepted, and she wrote up the contract we discussed.

The seller had offered the washer and dryer in the listing as being negotiable items, indicating they might remain with the property. The other agent said nothing about asking for the washer and dryer in her verbal terms, even though I asked several times if there were any other terms to her offer. But, she incorporated all the terms of the listing as a phrase inserted in the written offer. At the agreed price, my sellers did not want to include the washer and dryer, feeling they had been deceived. In order to complete the deal, I bought my sellers a new washer and dryer to solve the problem, and thought of the expense as a cost of my education. If you do not get everything clearly on the table when you are negotiating, you might have to pay for your mistake.

There is a reason why the National Association of REALTORS® has the standards of practice urging that everything be in writing. It avoids expensive educations.

6. Get Something in Return

If the other side wants to get a benefit, make sure you at least ask for something in return in order to stop people from continuing to grind you for more and more concessions. Simply ask, "If I can do that for you, what can you do for me?" If you leave it up to your counterpart to offer, you might get something more than what you would ask for. At a minimum, you will find out the value of this item to your counterpart. For example, if a buyer wants to extend the closing date for a sale and you represent the seller, at least you should be paid the holding costs—the amount it will cost your seller to hold the property for the additional time. You may also want to ask for any consequential costs, such as a loss of the use of the money they would get from the sale or any other cost. If there is no cost for the additional time, the buyer will think it is easy to come back and ask for another extension.

My nickname for this principle is "No Free Poker" from my son, Jeff. If you play poker with Jeff, he gets something in return when he plays a hand—you must either raise or fold, as there is "no free poker," according to him. When you visit **www.CreateAGreatDeal.com** and see that term, you will know the concept.

This policy is particularly important when dealing with modifications of contracts, as described above, and with tenants. If every time the tenant asks for something you do not ask for something in return, you will have an unending stream of requests. For example, one of my tenants wanted to be late with the rent, as they had a cash flow glitch, and they wanted me to waive the late fee. I allowed them to be late but insisted they pay the late fee and take care of an issue I had with the back yard. A sub-principle is never waive a late fee or any other benefit you are entitled to, but collect it later or add it to what is settled up at the end of the tenancy.

Think of this principle as making a trade-off and getting something in return for your concession. Exchanging a concession that has less value to you and more value to your counterpart enhances the deal from their standpoint: We will give you a better price if you will give us better terms. For example, if you want to buy a home with a contingency of selling your home, offer the seller a better price in return for your contingency terms. This gives the seller a reason to wait for you to sell your house, as the seller gets more money by giving you better terms. Also, you will probably sell your house for a higher price if you are not under extreme pressure to sell it to buy the other house (or lose your earnest money deposit) under a non-contingent contract.

Get something in return immediately and do not rely on your counterpart remembering to repay your favor later. Most people in a real estate transaction have an attitude that asks, "What have you done for me in the last five minutes?" If it has been longer than five minutes, the value of what you did has decreased dramatically. For example, every time I represent a seller who gives a buyer a low price, I make the buyer's agent promise that they will not ask for anything other than the absolute minimum when it comes to repairs. I can count on one hand the number of times that the other agent honors that promise. So, do not get your seller to count on the buyer asking for minimal repairs in this situation, because they will be disappointed. In fact, get them ready for the buyer to ask for everything, and your clients will rarely be surprised.

7. Reciprocity

You can consider this idea as the reverse of Get Something In Return: You give something first in order to get something back. You may remember the Hare Krishnas looking for a donation at the airport. They would give you a flower before they asked for the donation. Men have been buying women drinks and dinner for centuries, hoping to get lucky. One of the mainstays of our society is that if someone gives you something, you owe them something. If you want to read more on this idea, as well as many other ways to deal with the psychology of influence, read Robert Cialdini's *Influence, The Psychology of Persuasion.* His story about buying tickets to the sanitation workers' ball is priceless, as he wonders how he was influenced into buying tickets to an event he did not want to attend that would be full of people he would not want to meet.

If you are at an impasse in your negotiations, offer the other side something in an effort to break the logjam. They may give you what you need in return.

I was trying to close a sale on a property in Cary, North Carolina, where my seller was being stubborn in refusing to do reasonable repairs. The buyer was getting upset and preparing to walk away. The house had serious issues; and would be extremely hard for me to sell again.

There was an issue with the air conditioning system that had been inspected during a hot spell in the fall. When the weather turned cold again, we could not get the air conditioning contractor to test or repair the system. I had to get some trust from the buyer and the buyer's agent. The buyer had asked to have flooring installed in the attic over the garage, a completely ridiculous request when you are supposed to be asking for existing items that are broken to be repaired. There was no reason the seller should install flooring where there was none. I used to be a builder, and I spent from four o'clock in the afternoon to 10:45 at night flooring this attic. Now the buyer and the buyer's agent felt he owed me something. So, I asked that they meet me and my air conditioning contractor at the property.

The air conditioning contractor laughed before the meeting, saying this was the first time in 26 years of business that he was going to inspect and repair an air conditioning system in 45 degree weather. We showed the buyer and his agent that the system appeared to work well, and tested what we could. It could not be recharged with Freon at this temperature, so the buyer would have to take the risk of some cost for fixing the system next spring, as it might need some work. Since he had gotten his floored attic so his eight-year-old son could not open the door from the bonus room and fall through the ceiling joist, he took on a risk he might not have done otherwise.

If you are using reciprocity, try to establish some common ground or appreciation with the other side first. In the preceeding example, I found out that this buyer who wanted the floored attic used to work in construction. So did I. I had him and his agent help me carry the plywood to the attic when we met at the property, and we got to exchanging construction stories as we worked together. There is something about working on a project together that helps relationships. Since he could see that I had something in common with him, we were able to relate more with a feeling of trust when it came time to negotiate the remaining repairs. If you look hard enough, you will find a way to forge a connection with anyone.

8. Let Silence Do the Heavy Lifting

In her book, *Fierce Conversations,* Susan Scott gets the point across with "Let silence do the heavy lifting." Make your proposal, then SHUT UP! Most Americans cannot stand silence, so your counterpart will say something. If you remain silent, they will say something else. Let them respond to your offer, and if you want to see if you can get something else out of them at that point, just wait and see if they offer more.

Most people think they have to learn what to say to be persuasive. It is much more effective to learn when to say nothing, to be absolutely still, in order to get things moving in the direction you want. As real estate becomes more international, you will deal with people from different cultures, and you will learn that they use silence much more than Americans do, as they have found that Americans are not comfortable with silence.

Silence is also particularly useful when the other side has made you angry with their latest statement. Instead of lashing back, just be quiet. If they are at all sensitive, they will pick up on your feelings and possibly change their position instead of dealing with your wrath. With my Irish temper, this was particularly difficult to learn. After enough times where an angry outburst ruined everything, I learned that silence could accomplish more.

> *I was standing at the microphone in front of the Planning Commission of the City of Rancho Palos Verdes, representing a proposed real estate development, when Planning Commissioner John McTaggert asked if we would make some outrageous concession to the neighbors who opposed the project. John is a wonderful man, a long-time friend whose public service I admire, but he and I frequently disagree on what a government can take from a developer. He could tell from the long pause*

before I answered that I was upset and trying to calm down. As I paused, he followed up with, "Of course that is something we could not require, so I guess you would not consider that." All I had to do was agree with his last statement, and the negotiation on that point was over.

Silence is particularly important after a "Flinch" reaction to someone's first proposal, or when you use the "Vise" technique by saying "You'll have to do better than that!" You will learn all about the Flinch and Vise in Chapter 10. If you keep talking, it takes the pressure away from your counterpart to respond. Just flinch to physically show a reaction that their proposal is foolish, then let the silence do the heavy lifting and wait for the response.

The counter-measure to silence is more silence. Some people believe that the person who talks first loses, but I think that approach is just a game. My favorite response is to ask a question in response to their question. I have not broken under the silence by giving them an answer, but I ended the awkward moment. If there is more than one person you are dealing with, you can always end the silence by starting to talk with the other person.

9. Ask Questions

In his book, *Negotiate Like the Pros*, John Patrick Dolan says that questions are the most powerful tool of an expert negotiator. Questions let you find out what is important to either your client or your counterpart, and (as we know) knowledge is power. Listen carefully to the answers instead of working on what you are going to say next, because the best negotiators are not smooth talkers but good listeners.

In *Weekend Millionaire Secrets to Negotiating Real Estate*, Mike Summey and Roger Dawson give four techniques for asking open-ended questions, the ones that get your counterpart to give more information than just "yes" or "no." The first technique is to repeat what they said as a question. They say, "We want a quick closing"; you say, "You want a quick closing?" and be quiet. Let them tell you why. If you ask "Why do you want a quick closing?" it sounds more confrontational. Using this phrasing is a more graceful way to learn the reasons behind their request.

The second technique is to ask about feelings, that is, how they felt about what was said or what happened. When a seller has their listing expire, ask how they felt about that. You will probably get a litany of everything the other real estate agent should have done to get it to sell.

The third technique is a derivative of the second. Ask for the person's reaction to what happened. When the mortgage broker says several lenders would not place your buyer's loan at the interest rate they wanted, ask "What is your reaction to that?" You will get an explanation of what happened along with suggestions for what to do.

The fourth technique is to ask for a restatement. Your buyer says they want to make a ridiculously low offer. You indicate that you need to understand what is important about making such a low offer. You will get an explanation of the logic behind the proposed number.

I have a fifth technique. I ask, "What would you do if you were in my shoes?" It gets an explanation of the justification of the other person's position, and gets them to look at the situation from your point of view.

Ron Shapiro and Mark Jankowski have excellent questioning techniques in *The Power of Nice*. They agree with technique four above—that if you want your counterpart to go into more detail, ask for a restatement of their idea so they can explain it in different terms. Many times, in addition to getting more information you will also get a slight change in their position. You will need to phrase this in your own style, as asking for a restatement sounds more like a lawyer than a real estate agent. Instead of my technique of asking what the counterpart would do if they were in my shoes, these authors propose asking your counterpart to show you how a particular idea would work. When they have to explain how it would work for you, they are forced to see it from your perspective. Another way to question is to ask "who says" it has to be that way when your counterpart makes a particular demand. You might find out there is a difference of opinion among the people you are negotiating with—or there is someone else who is mandating a particular result.

I have learned a lot of these lessons by mistakes, and I try not to repeat them. So, ask questions, listen carefully, then ask follow-up questions to focus on the responses to those questions.

> I had clients coming from New York, referred to me by past clients. The lady of the house felt she knew it all. She gave me a price range and would not allow any discussion of why. When I tried to ask what was the basis of her price limit, she would not discuss it, and she would not work with my lenders to review her figures. If she had not been referred to me by a past client, I would not have put up with this behavior. But my policy is to always make my past clients look good when they refer their friends to me.
>
> I found her family a home in Holly Springs, North Carolina, that was in the specified price range and had all the other features she wanted. We met the builder and his agent at the home and negotiated the sale in a round table style of negotiations, standing around the island in the kitchen. We signed the contract, and on the way out to their car, her husband asked me what their monthly payments would be. She tried to stop the discussion, as she felt she knew it all. I did a quick calculation,

and mentioned the amount of the property taxes and insurance, then started to add them on my PDA.

She turned ashen white. She had greatly over-estimated the property taxes, as New York taxes are much higher than North Carolina property taxes. They had settled for much less house to stay within what she thought was her monthly budget. I told them the contract could be terminated, as there were contingencies we could use. Instead, we negotiated with the builder to finish off an unfinished attic and got everything they wanted in the home and still stayed below the budget. Since I had not done my questioning homework, I almost negotiated the wrong result. As a result of this experience, I insist that the buyers who work with my team get a "good faith estimate" from a lender for all of their monthly payments and closing costs, and we question our buyers on any assumptions they may be making concerning their payments.

10. More Effort Means More Attachment

The more work someone has done on a deal, the more attached they will become to making a deal. If there is no commitment of time and energy, it is easy to walk away. If you have spent days researching, offering, countering, and negotiating, you will probably put in more effort and stretch more on the terms in order to put it together.

In *Tips & Traps When Negotiating Real Estate*, Robert Irwin devotes a chapter to discussing how advantageous it is to get your counterpart and their clients to invest time in negotiating. His discussion also points out how negotiating items one at a time is advantageous for the person making the offer, which is the reason behind my principle of getting everything on the table before you start negotiating so that the other party cannot drag you into a long process.

Make the other agent invest some time and effort in an offer and you increase the chances that they will work on it until a deal is made. For example, sometimes agents who make verbal offers on my listings call to say, "You are asking $1,400,000 for that home in Rancho Palos Verdes, will they take $1,200,000?" If you present that offer, the buyer and the buyer's agent have no time invested in making it, so if it is not accepted outright, they are more likely to walk away. Since the National Association of REALTORS® Code of Ethics does not allow you to quote any price other than the one in the Multiple Listing Service, you have an easy way to refuse to answer. Then you can mention the policy of having all the terms of an offer in writing, which helps to get them to write up an offer. During the time they research and write the offer, the clients start to visualize themselves moving into the home and mentally arrange their furniture and life in that house. The written offer is presented, and when they get a counter offer, it is more likely that they will continue the negotiations.

By the way, if you are a buyer's agent, making a verbal offer is the best way to show that you are not serious about a house. It is an invitation to the seller to pay you no respect in considering your offer. If it is not even worth your time to write it down, how good is it? The seller will think that if you won't even write it down, you must think the offer is ridiculous. If you want to buy something, treat the seller with respect and present a written offer. Less effort means less probability of success.

You need to be aware of this effect on you and your client in negotiations. If you have spent a long time and tremendous effort in negotiating, it is more likely that you will make concessions just to get something out of the effort. However, you should realize that the time and effort are gone, whether you make a deal or not. So just keep a balanced view of the deal, or you will stretch more than you should to make a deal you should not make.

11. Walk Away Slowly

If you are going to take your other choice, let the other side know by using something like a trial balloon. Indicate you are going to withdraw your offer, but do not run away so fast that they cannot catch up to you and make you an offer that will make you stay in the deal. For example, I have heard that some small hotels and inns in Italy negotiate their room rates dramatically. If you start to walk away, the desk clerk will follow you to try to make a deal. Some negotiators measure how good a deal they made by how far away from the hotel they are when they decide that they will accept the offer.

The more you convince your counterpart that you have the ability to walk away, the more powerful you are in the negotiations. That reason is why it is important to keep improving your other choice, so that your counterpart can feel your willingness to walk away.

Danyelle Holland was a wonderful buyer's agent for my Team For YOUr Dreams in Raleigh, North Carolina. She had a buyer who purchased a house where the siding was in terrible shape. The seller was only obligated to repair the siding that was currently damaged, which was about 30 percent of the surface area. But our inspector made it clear that it would not be long before the rest of the siding would fail, so our buyers would be better off getting it all replaced. The North Carolina contract says the siding is fine if it "is not in need of immediate repair." The remainder of the siding was not in need of immediate repair, but it would be within a year or two. Danyelle had asked the sellers to give an allowance to replace all the siding, and the sellers properly said no. She called me to ask what to do. I said to Walk Away Slowly.

Danyelle prepared the necessary forms for the buyer to terminate the contract and sent them to the seller, as we had another contingency for the cost of the repairs that would allow us to terminate. The seller needed to close on this house to buy their other house, or else they might be stuck with two mortgages if they lost this sale. We also presented to the seller that once this sale fell through, they would be back on the market as "damaged goods," as the real estate agent community would realize there was something wrong with the house and the seller might well have to replace all the siding anyway to sell it. The sellers "caught up to us" before we completely walked away and made us a much better offer to fund nearly all of the siding and all the other repairs.

Note that this tactic is different from a bluff. Some real estate agents like to bluff. I don't. You will be working with the same real estate agents over and over. If they learn that you bluff, none of your proposals will get respect. My son Jeff's poker experience teaches me a lot. He bluffs so often that you never know if he has a hand or not. He even wears a shirt that says "I Never Bluff," but no one at the table believes the shirt. My daughter, Laurie, plays poker differently, and when she bets, you figure she has a hand. As a result, on the rare occasions when she bluffs, she pushes all the other players out of the hand and wins the pot with a lousy hand.

12. Maintain Your Credibility

There is no one sale that is worth damaging your credibility. Even within one sale, if you lose your credibility at some stage, no one will believe you throughout the rest of the sale. I love the saying, "The difficult thing about a liar is that occasionally he tells the truth." Once you are a liar, no one will believe you when you tell the truth.

> *I represented a young couple buying their first house, and they had limited financing available. We made an offer where the seller was represented by a top RE/MAX agent in Raleigh, North Carolina. My clients needed to negotiate the price down in order to afford the property.*
>
> *We made a good offer on Friday, but the seller's agent was out of town. When I got a call from her, she said she would not be able to respond until Monday; she was expecting another offer to come in by then, and she wanted to wait to see if it came in before responding to our offer. I told her if we did not have a response by Saturday at 5 p.m., our offer was withdrawn. I had discussed this strategy with my clients as part of our game plan, as we could not let other offers be presented and still get the low price we needed. She said she would see what her clients wanted to do.*
>
> *When the other agent called me the following Monday to say the other offer had not come in, and her clients wanted to give us a counter offer, I explained that we had purchased another house on Sunday. I have had several sales since then with her, and she always believes that I am going to do what I say I will do. All the other sales have gone well, and she even wrote a letter of recommendation for me.*

You will not hurt your relationship with other real estate agents by doing what you say you are going to do, even if you are doing something that is not favorable for them.

13. Watch for "Tells" and Take It All In

If you watch people, they will tell you everything—usually not with what they say, but with how they say it and how they react to what is said. Look, listen, and fully absorb the behavior and body language of your counterpart; she is trying to tell you how to put the deal together.

Poker is great training for negotiating, as it teaches you about "Tells." A Tell is some behavior that lets you see what a person is really thinking and feeling. If your counterpart is saying she is completely confident that her buyers have the financing all arranged, but she is sitting forward with her shoulders hunched up, her face flushed, her hands animated, and her voice at a higher pitch than the rest of what she says, you know there is no confidence there.

"It is better to remain silent and be thought a fool than to open your mouth and remove all doubt" is a quote so popular that is attributed to Abraham Lincoln, Mark Twain, and Samuel Johnson. Heed the advice and don't be busy talking, be busy watching and listening. Listen to what is actually being presented, not just what you want to hear. Don't follow what most people do as described in Paul Simon's song *The Boxer* that "A man hears what he wants to hear and disregards the rest." Get your emotional filters out of the way so you really hear, see, and understand what is being presented to you, not only by your counterpart but also by your clients.

Work on understanding the person you are dealing with before you try to get them to understand you. Since the person with the most knowledge of the other person's wants and needs will do the best in the negotiations, let them go first, ask open-ended questions to help them along, do not interrupt, and take in all the information. To be sure you understand their position, repeat back what you hear to see if you have it right, then just listen again. While you are repeating it back, give some affirming reaction to show that you have empathy for their position, even if you disagree with it.

While you are observing and listening, look the other person in the eye, as it makes you seem attentive and trustworthy while at the same time letting you judge their eye movements to see if they are saying what they mean. Do not make them uncomfortable by staring, but look at their eyes most of the time.

14. Use Objective Information and Expert Opinion

The use of objective information makes your position look more reasonable, and it is easier for your counterpart to present and understand your position. For example, your client has an opinion of value, and your counterpart's client has another opinion of value. What do you do to get them to agree? Use comparable values to show what an objective interpretation of the value would be. Real estate works on the Principle of Substitution: one property can be a substitute for another, as they all provide some of the features buyers want. The price at which buyers will change their interest in one property to another is the price point where the two properties substitute for each other. So, provide information about similar sales to show that the property in question is worth a comparable value to the similar sale. If you have a good reason for your offer, your counterpart will not feel that you are trying to take advantage of them.

Dianne Dunn, a real estate agent from New Bern, North Carolina has a great example of how to do this. She says, "I have included a Buyer's Agent cover letter to the listing agent with an offer several times. In the cover letter we have complimented the seller on the finer points of the home, and then listed the reasons for the buyer's offer (needs updated carpeting, repainting, etc.). I've also attached a current Comparative Market Analysis, showing where the buyer's offer price was established, if it's much lower than the listing price. In the letter, we encourage the listing agent to pass along any of this information to the seller. If this is carefully prepared, without insulting anyone, it can be a useful tool to the listing agent who could not get their sellers to reduce a price."

Watch out for comparisons based on price per square foot. They do not take into account features like front porches, vaulted ceilings, two story family rooms, and other amenities that do not add to the useable square footage. Also, the comparison only works if the homes are similar size, as small homes sell for more per square foot than do big homes. A small home has a kitchen and a couple of baths, which are the expensive parts of a house, then additional rooms. A big house has a kitchen and a couple of baths, then more rooms or more spacious rooms. Since the additional area in the bigger home is less expensive to build, homes of similar quality with substantially more square footage sell for less per square foot than much smaller homes. If you are comparing homes where the square feet varies by 10 percent, the comparison has some validity. But, if you are comparing homes of dramatically dissimilar size, you will get numbers that are way off. So, when a rookie agent tells you that your much smaller home is selling for too much because the price per square foot is out of line with the much bigger homes in the neighborhood, just smile.

Some of the best situations in which to use objective information are in pricing a listing and on price reductions. For some analytical clients, it may be enough to show them a graphic of the listings of the homes for sale that they are competing with (some of which could be priced in Fantasyland) and the ones that actually sold. You might also show them the number of actual buyers in certain price ranges, which is particularly important in luxury homes, as one price point may be selling much better than another. If your sellers do not get the point by looking at the printed listings, show them their competition in real life by taking them through the properties. Negotiating the proper price with the seller is the precursor to getting an offer so you can negotiate the price with the buyer.

If you get to a real impasse, you might call in an expert and agree to use their opinion as objective information. This can be helpful in repair issues, where the buyer and seller disagree about the condition of the property. For example, there are some small cracks in the foundation that the buyer thinks are structural, but the seller thinks they are minor. If you call in a respected structural engineer, the opinions give way to science, and then you can deal with the objective information. If it is structural, you fix it or cancel the sale. If it is minor, you give the buyer the comfort of the written opinion with the engineer's seal that can be used when the buyer wants to re-sell the property.

15. Eliminate Useless Objections

If an objection is made or a limit is proposed, test it immediately. It may go away. If you accept the objection or limit and start to work on the sale with that limit, you will be stuck with it. If you question it immediately, you might find out there is some flexibility, or that the problem does not really exist. This technique is also a way to not let other people's problems become your problems. If the seller's objection is that the purchase price does not give him enough money to pay off his credit card debts, explain that the value of the home has nothing to do with his credit cards, because the buyer does not care what the seller is going to do with the money.

For example, your client says they can only afford monthly payments of $1,600, which will not be enough for the kind of house they are describing. Immediately ask what your lender told them was the maximum they could qualify for. If it is $2,200, and they were just trying to be frugal, ask what is more important, getting the home they want or keeping the payments at $1,600. When the lady of the house says they want the home of their dreams, the acceptable payment is usually increased.

16. Give Partners Alone Time

When it is time to make a decision, you can sometimes help most by getting out of the way. When you can see that a couple really likes the house you are in, and you have answered their questions, find a way to excuse yourself so that they can talk privately for a few minutes. This practice applies to married partners, business partners, or anyone else with any type of a relationship. They are more comfortable with each other than they will ever be with you. A moment of private discussion where they solidify their interest will do more than anything you can say.

> *Bill and Jo Marie were interested in buying a new home from a national builder, and Bill is an excellent negotiator. We had a game plan to get certain features in the house, and we wanted a discount price. Before our meeting, we sent the builder a spreadsheet of what we wanted and the price we would pay. We did the best we could, but there came a point where, after meeting with all the builder's sales staff and executives, we could not get them to match Bill's terms. Jo Marie wanted the house; Bill wanted to get the proper terms. I left them alone for about ten minutes to discuss what to do; they decided to buy the house, as they wanted their children to grow up in this neighborhood.*

17. Don't Let Little Things Stand In Your Way

I did not graduate from high school. I graduated from Pomona College and UCLA Law School. When I was a junior in high school, I met Bill Wheaton, the Director of Admissions for Pomona College, who asked me, "Why don't you apply to go to Pomona College next year?" It was a prestigious school, and I wanted to go there. I said the reason was because I was only a junior. His response has guided much of my life, "You shouldn't let little things like that stand in your way." So, I applied, I was admitted, and I skipped my senior year of high school.

If you have a buyer or a seller who wants to put something together but there is a "little thing" standing in the way, write up the offer with the item as a contingency. If the sellers will sell but they are worried about buying another home in a red hot seller's market, write up the sale with a contingency for the seller acquiring another house. If the buyer wants to buy but is concerned about the condition of the roof, write up the sale with a contingency for the roof passing a particular inspection. Big decisions are hard for some people to make, but you can get them to commit to a contract that has a condition in it, as they are not making the entire commitment all at once. By the time the contingency is evaluated, they will have accepted the commitment to the sale, and all they will have to deal with is the contingency.

18. Obey the Law, the Codes, and Your Gut Feelings

This suggestion seems so obvious when you are quietly reading this book, but in the heat of the moment, you might be tempted to "cut a corner." Be sure to let the law, the code of ethics, and that bad feeling in your gut stop you. Following these standards makes these decisions easy and stress free. You do not have to debate about the right action to take when a client wants to conceal a defect and tries to stop you from disclosing items in an inspection report. If you wonder, "Should I disclose this?' the answer is "Yes, you should."

Any client who wants you to lie or cheat does not value you as a counselor, so you have already lost their future business. Even more dangerous to your well-being is that this type of client is the first one to turn on you if there is a problem. Even worse, if they send you all their friends, you will spend too much of your life dealing with liars and cheats. So do not tell your client that you did not hear something, that you are going to ignore a defect, or that you were not part of a discussion. Just do what the law and the codes of ethics require.

Pay attention to that feeling in your gut. It is trying to tell you something important. If you feel that you cannot trust someone, you are probably right. No deal and no client are worth risking your reputation and your license. Besides, cutting the corner will only make the problem worse.

> *When I sold my house in California in 2008, my supplement to the Transfer Disclosure Statement and other disclosure documents went on for pages and pages. It was so long, it was boring. But the form asked if anything on the house had been repaired, and I had owned the house since 1975 and completely remodeled it several times, so there was a lot of detail to present. The buyers thanked me for all that information which made it easier for them to take the property "as is."*

19. Know the Limits of E-mail, Fax, and Telephone

Many negotiating techniques were developed by people engaged in business meetings and round table discussions. They evolved for use when you are meeting face-to-face. You have to adjust them for modern real estate negotiating, most of which is done by phone, fax, email, and text messaging. I have clients from California who buy investment properties in Raleigh, North Carolina, who I have never seen face-to-face; we communicate over the phone and by email.

Most of the way we judge communication is by the tone of voice and body language; the least important factor is the words that are said. I communicate much better in person, so writing this book has been harder than teaching seminars, so come see me face to face to get the full effect. Using email, text messaging, fax, or telephone eliminates some of the most important clues that we use to communicate.

Email and text messaging

With email and text messaging, there is no tone or body language, so be careful that you are not misunderstood, particularly when you are kidding. Use emoticons like ;-) to try to add some tone. Also, never send an email that you would not want to have sent to everyone in the world, because it just might end up forwarded to a discussion group. I had to learn this the hard way, after sending an email to a Rancho Palos Verdes city councilman when I was angry over the effect of the council's discussions of a geological issue on my neighborhood's real estate values. He forwarded it to all the members of the council and the planning staff. Luckily, the council understood.

When you write an email, you need to go into more detail to be sure you get your message across, as you cannot look at the person's face to see if they are following you. You do not get the question-and-answer interchange to help focus your discussion. An advantage, and disadvantage, of email is that it leaves a written record, so if you want to be able to prove that something was sent or said, email is wonderful. If you need to "spin" a conversation in a different direction, however, having the email record will make it harder to "spin." And if you are worried about making a big mistake, do not do it in writing in an email.

Fax

Do not try to communicate by fax; it should be used only for sending documents. There are exceptions to this rule, such as sending a proposal to a bank's Loss Mitigation Department when you are negotiating a "short sale." Since the loss mitigation negotiator will rarely talk to you and requires all the documents by fax, the transmittal sheet is the only chance you have to tell your story.

Telephone

It is easier to say "no" over the phone than it is face-to-face, as you do not have to be involved as much in the other person's reaction, and you can end the conversation more quickly. So if you want to turn someone down, call. If you want to increase your chances of getting a "yes," take the time to have a face-to-face meeting.

People are more in a hurry over the phone, as there is some force that wants to get the conversation finished. To take advantage of this, prepare an outline of what you want to discuss, get your presentation down, then call. You can be fully prepared when you catch your counterpart unprepared with a phone call. Then use their tendency to rush to a conclusion to your advantage. To counteract this when you are caught unprepared, screen your calls with caller ID or find some reason to call them back. If you can find out what they want to discuss, arrange to call them back after you are completely prepared.

You still get the advantage of tone in telephone conversations, so use all your personality to your advantage. When I was starting my practice in North Carolina, we could call the expired listings over the phone. I was able to make a large number of appointments over the phone, and got 90 percent of the listings when I met with them. With the "do not call" regulations in effect, I get many less opportunities to meet with sellers of expired listings, as my mailings are not as effective as my voice.

Silence is a wonderful tool for telephone calls. It can do "the heavy lifting" when you are meeting face-to-face, but it is even more impressive over the telephone. Since the only information your counterpart has is the sound on your end of the phone, being totally silent creates a great reaction. When someone presents bad news, I respond by a lengthy silence, looking for them to back down from the bad position. At a minimum, the silence will get the other party to jump in with some additional information, normally to soften what they just said.

Distractions kill negotiations. When you are working over the telephone, do not let people coming into your office or the ding of incoming email distract you as you concentrate on the negotiations.

When you discuss face-to-face, you can see the "wind-up before the pitch" in your counterpart's face, and you can be prepared for important points. On the phone, you only get the importance of what was said after it is said.

One of the advantages of face-to-face negotiations is that you can look at the same documents and exchanging materials. Modern technology has made it possible for you and your counterpart to send materials immediately, however, so you can both look at the same thing. Thank goodness for Adobe Acrobat and the pdf format—you can convert a word processed document to a pdf before you send it, so your counterpart cannot alter it. If you want to be even more connected, there are programs that will allow you to look at your counterpart's computer screen, and even control that screen, so highlighting materials, pointing out certain parts, and drawing diagrams can take place when you are on the phone.

After you have concluded a telephone negotiation, you may want to confirm it in writing to create a record. I always take notes when I am talking on the phone, so transcribing the notes into an email is easy. In North Carolina, counter offers are verbal, so go over all the terms as a summary to the conversation so that your counterpart will convey every one of the terms properly. When an agreement is reached in North Carolina, I discuss all the revisions to the contract in detail so that the changes to be made to the contract will be correct the first time, and we can avoid having to modify the document again.

I learned this the hard way with an agent who had gotten nearly all the terms right. He ran all over town to get his client to sign and initial the contract. The one item he forgot was to change the interest rate on the finance contingency. I did not want to send him back to his clients at ten o'clock at night to make this change, so I had my clients sign the contract with the understanding that the buyer would correct this oversight. The buyer later terminated the contract, using the unreasonably low interest rate in the finance contingency after the buyer's agent had failed to get the interest rate in the contract revised.

When it comes to contracts, no good deed goes unpunished. No matter how rude it may seem, make the other agent get the contract perfect before you allow your client to sign it, as the other agent has no motivation to get it right if your seller has already signed the contract.

Be careful of voice mail—just ask Alec Baldwin. I do not leave bad news on a voice mail, because it should be discussed personally to show more consideration for the person's reaction. With some extremely busy agents, you have no choice but to leave everything you need in the voice mail message, as you will not get a chance to communicate with them personally in a timely manner. I have done several counter offers and reached sales agreements negotiating by voice mail with mega-agents in North Carolina. But if you are competing with a mega-agent for a listing, emphasize your communication skills and your availability for personal contact--that the seller will not "feel like a number" with you. To prove your point, have the seller call the mega-agent and listen to the voice mail message that says they only return calls at certain times of the day.

Now that you have the principles to guide you through the negotiating process, you need to learn the rules.

CHAPTER 8

RULES OF REAL ESTATE NEGOTIATING

There are certain rules of negotiating that will greatly increase your success if you know when to follow them—and when to break them. Learning how to take the rules to the limit and bend—if not break—them is key to successful negotiating.

1. No Hostile Emotions

One of the functions of a real estate agent is to be a shock absorber, to keep your client's emotions from agitating the other side, or vice versa. You also need to keep any hostile feelings you possess from poisoning the interaction. When you are negotiating over a home, both the buyers and sellers are under stress. The sellers are giving up what has been the center of their world, and the buyers are trying to establish a new place that will reflect their status, values, and ego. The amount of money to be gained or lost is huge compared to what they normally deal with. Since it is difficult to get an accurate value for any house, you are dealing with a seller who thinks its worth is more than she is being offered and a buyer who thinks its worth is really less than what she is being asked to pay. Put this against a background where each side fears "being taken," and you get lots of emotion.

At some stage, the personalities of the parties may not mesh, which can create a charged atmosphere. You need to have grace under pressure. One way to maintain that grace is to convince yourself that if you let the others make you angry, they conquer you by eliminating your ability to control the situation. Do not give them that victory.

I have a strong Irish temper, so it is hard for me not to describe what a "south end of a north-bound horse" the other party is being. But if I allow myself to say something obnoxious, then my riled-up client will react by trying to beat the other side instead of trying to put the sale together. When anger takes over, the counterparts stop focusing on logic and rational self-interest to focus instead on how to harm the other party.

Focus on the fact that you cannot control the other party's behavior, but you can control your reaction to it. Instead of thinking that your counterpart is difficult, realize your contribution to the difficulty and deal with your own behavior. If you change from being an adversary to being a partner, the cooperation will allow you to collaborate on a better result.

This idea is particularly critical at the beginning of negotiations. What you say in the beginning sets the tone for how things are going to proceed. If you start out arguing, your counterpart will figure that there is no chance for a Win-win/collaborative negotiation and will move into a win-lose mode. So, don't argue, persuade.

Ron Shapiro and Mark Jankowski emphasize the importance of this concept in *Bullies, Tyrants and Impossible People*, which follows their *Power of Nice*. The **N** in Nice stands for neutralize emotions, which I believe to be the most important part of the process, and why it is first. To avoid a hostile reaction, rivet your focus on the issues so that you will act smartly, instead of react viscerally. You can also develop certain physiological changes, such as Mr. Jankowski's technique of putting a finger across his lips when confronted to remind him to be quiet while he controls his emotions and thinks before he responds. Taking a few deep breaths, changing the pace of your speech, and talking in a lowered tone are all good techniques to de-escalate emotions.

You have to keep hostilities out of the process not only during initial negotiations but also all the way through the closing. If you let emotions flare, negotiations that started as Win-win can quickly change to win-lose, with one side wanting to dominate the other. The result is normally a disaster, as even if you get the beginning of the sale together, the remaining stages will be done in the same win-lose atmosphere, so the negotiations on repairs and any other issues are much more likely to make the sale fall apart. Revenge does no one any good, even though it is so tempting.

I had a sale in Raleigh where the inexperienced agent thought her obligation was to be contentious and to battle every issue. It is prudent to examine every issue, but you do not need to create a battle, as we can disagree without being disagreeable.

On her advice, her sellers refused to do most of the repairs requested by my Team's client. All of the repairs were typical items, clearly proper to be done under the contract. At first, the agent tried to say that the sellers could not afford to do them, but we checked with the closing attorney and found that the sellers were making a profit and would get a check for more than $50,000 on the sale of the house. She battled every little issue, just so she could show her clients a victory on items that would save them small amounts of money. These communications were frequently done in writing, so we had to forward them to our clients instead of being able to relay a non-emotional message involving just the issues.

The buyers nearly walked away. The sale was delayed. The buyers did not accept the home in its condition at the walk-through before closing because they had been treated so poorly. They would have let the problems go if they had been treated well. After the closing, the agent for the buyers was talking to her clients in the parking lot, saying she was so glad she was able to "win this dog fight" for them. After she left, I overheard her clients talking; the selling wife said to her husband, "How stupid does she think we are? She made this a miserable experience, we fell for her recommendation to try to save a couple of dollars and it cost us hundreds, not to mention the heartache. Who knows who won this dog fight, but I certainly got bit more than I wanted." The clients are not looking for a dogfight; they are looking to work with everyone else and get the sale closed gracefully.

Concentrate on the sale and the issues in the sale. Then try to deal pleasantly with the personalities involved. The personalities are a temporary problem, while buying or selling the house is the long-term result.

A corollary to this rule is to use positive emotions to encourage a sale. Homes are bought on emotion. Women have more influence in the buying decision, so concentrate more on their feelings. Play to the emotion that causes a bond to the home. Encourage this affection because it will help the negotiations. I once gave a letter to a buyer's agent with my counter offer for a property, and in it I commended the buyer for some of the work their family had done for the community, as he was in politics. In response to my letter, I received a letter with a counter offer from the buyer saying how she had driven by the house I was selling for about a year, hoping it could be hers. When it was vacant, she and her son would go into the back yard and play catch after peeking in the windows hoping to it could be theirs. We used this information to our advantage with every counter offer we made.

2. Don't Accept the First Offer

If you are dealing with another real estate agent or a professional negotiator, nearly always the first offer is not the best they will do. Give them a counter offer and see if they will do better. Or flinch and say they will have to do better than that, and see if they will improve the offer. One of the reasons not to accept the first offer is that the other party will immediately feel that they could have done better, a sensation commonly called the Winner's Curse. They will try to make up for that feeling either by trying to withdraw the offer or by getting some advantage later in the transaction.

Another reason not to accept the first offer is that the other party will think there must be something wrong with the property if you are not willing to risk the time and effort to see if you can do better by presenting a counter offer. People negotiate differently, just like they waltz differently. Some people like to waltz only a little, while others want to glide across the entire dance floor all night. But nearly everyone wants to dance some. If you accept the first offer, you do not give the other party the opportunity to dance.

One exception to the rule is when you are not dealing with experienced professionals. When I sold my last home in California, I received offers through a series of less-than-wonderful real estate agents. The first offers always stank, as the real estate agents were representing buyers who listened to the media instead of their real estate agent. These buyers thought the market was a raging buyers' market, but there was only a three-month supply of homes for sale in this area, which is actually a strong seller's market. I always gave the real estate agent a counter offer as a professional courtesy because I assume that the real estate agent is a professional negotiator. Many of them could not get their clients to go farther, though, so they ended the effort. Since I was not going to sell for their ridiculous first-offer price, I did not lose anything. This creates its own exception to the rule: If you are dealing with an untrained real estate agent, you have to adapt to their skill level, or lack thereof.

Another exception to the rule is when you know that the buyer is negotiating on more than one property. Older real estate agents are now shocked at this statement, but buyers will occasionally be pursuing more than one property at the same time, then go forward with the one that gives them the best deal. Particularly in California, there are so many contingencies to the contract a buyer can use to terminate the sale, that a sophisticated buyer may have several offers out at the same time. This technique is important in a raging seller's market, when you might have multiple offers out to buy every home, as it may take you many attempts to get to buy one house. If the price offered is close enough, and the amount to be gained by a counter offer is not worth the risk of losing the transaction, take the first offer. In this case, you must ask questions of the other agent, because you need to know whether the buyer has made multiple offers in order to consider breaking this rule. If you are a buyer's agent, you should be sure the listing agent knows there are multiple offers out, so that you can get a better deal for your client.

3. Do Not Accept the First "No"

For determined negotiators, "No" is merely an opening bargaining position.

This rule is particularly applicable when you are working with a bureaucracy, such as a government, banks, major builders, or insurance companies. If you go into the Planning Department for most governments in Southern California, their default answer is, "No, you cannot do that." If you believe that answer and do not apply for the permit you were seeking, they do not have to review the application. Thus they do not have to do any work, and they cannot be found to have done anything wrong, because nothing ever gets submitted for review. If the planner tells you that you can get a permit, and later that you cannot, the planner's mistake could hurt their career. So, the default answer is "No." Similarly, with Home Warranty insurance, if they can tell you, "No, it's not covered" and you go away, their problem is over.

I have developed a simple response: "I appreciate what you have to say, but that is the wrong answer." You have to say it with a smile, good tone of voice, and the right people skills so that you can get to a more serious review of what you want to accomplish. In other words, indicate that you are not going to be that easily dismissed.

Another part of this rule is when you run into someone who does not have the authority to say "Yes," find someone who does. Governmental organizations dealing with all sorts of real estate issues from property taxes to utility hook-ups to building permits have set up their organization so that the lower-level administrators do not have the authority, creativity, or flexibility to solve many of the problems. That notion makes sense, because if you run the organization with the lower-level employees having too much flexibility, you will get too many bizarre results. If you run into someone who cannot say "yes," move the discussion to a supervisory person who can. Find out the reasons behind the no, and you might make a deal.

I had a strange problem recording a subdivision on a tract for an ocean-front property of 37 acres in Los Angeles County. The tax assessor had made a mistake in drawing the tax maps, showing part of our property as belonging to an adjacent property. In other words, the map of their lot was incorrect because it included part of our land. The adjacent property had not paid its taxes for years, owing many thousands of dollars.

You can only record a subdivision map if you show that all of property taxes are paid for all of the property in the subdivision. The land in question was a sliver about 10-feet wide at the base of a 160-foot cliff, and it was covered with water part of the time, i.e. it was worthless. The assessor's first-line personnel said the only way we could record the map was to pay all the back taxes for all of the adjoining parcel. If we did that, there was no way to get the money back. The other choice was to re-draw the tax map, but that would not be able to be done for months, maybe even a year. The subdivi-sion map had to be recorded in less than 45 days, otherwise it expired, and six years of work would go to waste.

So I explained that "That is the wrong an-swer." But none of the people in the office had the authority to provide any relief. The County Supervisor's office put me in touch with people with enough authority in the tax office to autho-rize an emergency evaluation of the change in the tax map. The sliver of land was evaluated for its proportionate share of the back taxes. Because it was so worthless, I was given a bill for $19.95 for the back taxes. I had to stand in three lines at the tax collector's office to pay the bill. It took most of a day to get my $20 bill in the proper hands and get the right receipts. I saved the nickel that I got back as change, just to enjoy my brush with bureaucratic death. The tract map was recorded, and there are 25 mansions on the property today. Do not wilt in the face of the first "No."

4. Get the Other Party To Make the First Offer

This rule does not apply to most real estate negotiations, as the etiquette of who makes the first offer on a property in the Multiple Listing Service is well-established. The listing price is the first offer. However, for informal negotiations such as an offer on a property that is not formally listed for sale, let the other party mention the price first. They may present a number that is better for you than what you would have offered. This rule may also come up on ancillary negotiations on a real estate sale, such as a buyer asking the seller if they want to sell the refrigerator after the sales contract has been signed. Let the other party suggest the price.

> *My mother, Lorna, and my brother, Bruce, used this rule in buying a lot for my brother in Laurel Canyon outside of Los Angeles. The property had been inherited by the current owner, who had not done much research on the price. When my family members met with the seller, he asked what they wanted to offer. My family knows the rule, so they changed the subject then asked him what he was asking for the property. When he quoted a low price, Lorna confirmed several other terms so she looked like she was not jumping too quickly on the low price, then accepted slowly with some conditions.*

The exceptions to this rule are few, the primary one occurring when the other party knows the rule. If you want to go anywhere, someone has to make the first offer, so you may have to break the rule just to get things moving. If you want to get the other party to make the first offer, build them up as the expert in the area, saying that they know more about the subject than you do. "Since you sell more homes with this kind of hardboard siding, what do you think would be a fair reduction in the price for replacing the siding?" builds up the other agent as the expert. If they give a number that is much better than you expected, all you have to do is defer to their expertise.

Another exception to the rule is discussed in *Negotiation* from Harvard Business Essentials. They look at the first offer as an Anchor that serves as a reference point and sets the tone for the rest of the negotiations. This book states that there are studies that show that the outcome of the negotiations correlate to the first offer, such as the example cited in the discussion of the Split the Difference technique, where most people end up half-way between where they start the negotiations. They say it is smart to set an anchor with the first offer if you have a good idea of your counterpart's walk-away price. In other words, if you can predict the reaction to your first offer, you may want to make the first offer. Even this book says that if you do not have a good idea of your counterpart's walk-away price, do not make the first offer.

5. Accept Slowly

If you get an offer that is way too good, do not jump up and down and accept it with glee. The other party will realize their mistake and, if they do not withdraw it, will try to make up for it someplace else in the process of the sale.

Instead of immediately saying "I accept," question some of the terms, confirm that they include some other part of the real estate to be bought, then slowly indicate that you could grudgingly be persuaded to stretch to accept their proposal. Possibly ask if they will throw in something little just to get you to accept. The other party will think they did all right, instead of feeling like they gave everything away.

6. Greed: Pigs Get Fat, Hogs Get Slaughtered

If you take everything, there is going to be a problem that ruins the deal. The best illustration of this rule is the strike by the printers for the New York newspapers years ago. The union got such an amazing contract that the members were thrilled, but the contract was so costly to the newspapers that most of them went out of business, making the printers unemployed. They dominated the negotiations, but lost their jobs. So leave something for the other side, as they need to have a reason or the ability to complete the contract.

After negotiating the price way, way down on a house in Rolesville, North Carolina, the first-time buyers represented by my Team had an inspection that revealed the house had extensive siding problems. The sellers did not have any money coming out of the sale and no savings, so they could not put the money in to close the sale. The first-time buyers were getting 100 percent financing and the sellers were paying the closing costs out of the sale, so neither side had the money to fix the siding. The buyers got stubborn by saying they would not work with the sellers to build the repairs into the cost of the sale, as they wanted to keep the great price that they had bragged about to their parents. There was not enough money in the transaction for the real estate agents to take care of the problem out of their commissions. So, the sale fell apart because there was nothing in it for the seller.

An example of how to avoid being too greedy comes from sellers I represented who wanted to sell quickly and came way down on the price for a home in Apex, North Carolina. The agent representing the buyer was involved in her second sale, so she did not have a great deal of experience. The house had polybutylene plumbing, like all the other homes built in that era in Apex. The agent for the buyer freaked out, as she had no experience with this type of plumbing, which is the subject of a class action lawsuit. Most agents had dealt with it and relied on the fact that if there were two leaks in the plumbing, the settlement fund would pay for replacing all the plumbing in the house. In other words, there was a third-party guarantee if it leaked twice, which protected the buyer. The sellers were not obligated to replace the plumbing, as it was normal for that type of house and it did not leak. Particularly at the low price, the sellers were not inclined to pay for all new plumbing. The buyers were new to the United States, barely spoke English, and had nothing other than their inexperienced real estate agent to guide them. (Anyone who looks at www.Polybutylene.com will be scared to death of it, until they realize the website is run by a plumbing company that wants to convince you to replace the plumbing.)

We increased the sales price of the home, as it was being sold under market value, and gave the buyer a credit for most of the cost of replacing the plumbing. The appraisal still came in over the increased price, as the seller was more interested in moving quickly into retirement than getting top dollar. The buyer got a home with new plumbing, the seller got almost the same proceeds, and the inexperienced agent got an education.

A short corollary to this rule is to allow the other real estate agent and her clients to maintain some dignity. You will work in the real estate community over and over, as the other real estate agents are your repeat customers, selling your listings over and over. Do not humiliate them, even if they deserve it.

A second corollary to this rule is this is a great time to use "split the difference" as a closing move, so that you can meet your counterpart half-way and give them at least a little victory. If you have a little difference between the two sides, splitting the difference gives your counterpart at least half a victory by giving them half of the difference.

7. Test Objections to Avoid Unnecessary Problems

Some objections are conditions—for example, unless the property has a family room, the buyers do not want it. Others are just objections, that is, they will still buy the house even though they have to do a lot of work on the yard. There are a number of different questions to test the objection, such as "Why is that important to you?" "What will that do for you?" and "Would that stop you from proceeding with this house?" If you want to overcome the objection, phrase the last question in an "assumptive close" manner, such as "But that wouldn't stop you from buying this home, would it?" Be quiet, and listen carefully to the answer. If it is a condition that cannot be met, move on to another property or another deal. If it is just an objection, find out how important it is and adjust accordingly. There is no such thing as a perfect house, so get your buyers to expect that they will have at least two serious objections to any property. If you do not test the objection, you will take on problems that you do not deserve.

8. Create a Sense of Urgency

If your counterpart thinks they have forever to act, you will get a bad result most of the time. Fear of loss is a wonderful motivator, so give your counterpart a sense of urgency that they may lose the property to someone else. Let a buyer's agent know that another party is coming back to look at the house for the fourth time, then let them come to the conclusion that they should write up an offer quickly. Let the seller know that your buyer wants you to show them another home that just came on the market, so it might be wise to accept your counter offer.

It is much better to use indirect pressure to create a sense of urgency than a direct ultimatum. If you provide the information, and the other party draws the conclusion that they need to act, you gracefully get the desired result without a confrontation and the emotions it generates. If you give an ultimatum that the offer needs to be accepted by 3 p.m., you have the possibility of terminating the negotiations when it is not accepted. Backing down from an ultimatum ruins your credibility and makes you look like you are playing games. Let the others draw the conclusion that they need to move quickly.

> *When we bought our house in Raleigh, it was a strong seller's market, and the house was everything my wife wanted. Linda Craft was our agent, and she gave us clear statistics on how the market favored the sellers, as well as a price analysis to show how good the deal was on this house. That informatioin lead us to the conclusion that we would need to accept quickly. We found a way to fax our acceptance from the airport in Pittsburgh on our flight back, which would be easy now, but took some work in 1995. Instead of testing the seller with another counter offer, we accepted the price due to our feeling that it was urgent for us to accept before anyone else got the house Judy loved.*

The way to counteract the news that someone else is making an offer is to "slowly walk away." Indicate that if they have someone else who wants to give them a better proposal, they should listen—but, if it does not work out, please give you a call. When they call, your negotiating power is greatly increased. Listen to the way the urgency is presented to pick up clues on its veracity. Normally, if there is someone who will make a better offer, your counterpart would be off dealing with that offer instead of telling you about the possibility of a better offer.

9. Do Not Reward Bad Behavior

Have you ever noticed that you make a great deal of concessions to the most miserable people, trying to make them happy? Even though you do everything possible, they still are not happy. The first step is to try to deal with them by not rewarding their bad behavior, by doing your best, and asking for some recognition for your effort. If you do not get proper respect for your efforts, it is much better to learn early on that you are dealing with a "black hole," a phenomenon in astronomy where the hole sucks in all the energy from everything around it. So, if you have miserable, unhappy people who are not going to be satisfied no matter how much you do, get rid of them and move on to the next client.

> *I had to learn this the hard way, with a client who was so demanding that he took all my time. His house sold at a record high price, but when the buyer asked for reasonable repairs, this seller would do nothing. So I took care of the repairs. When the buyer wanted to close early and save the seller money, this seller wanted additional compensation because it did not match his time schedule for closing. So I negotiated additional compensation when none was due. The seller decided I had not done enough, so he wanted some of my commission. When I did not give him everything he wanted, he was furious. Selling a home at a record high price in a declining market, after helping him buy it at a record low price, was not enough. I closed the sale and I have never had to talk to him again.*

Get away from the "black hole" before it sucks all the life out of you. The "black hole" will tell all his friends not to work with you, which is great, as you do not want to work with more people like that.

10. If You Shoot at a King, You Have to Kill Him

The phrase comes from a story I heard at the Palace of Versailles in France. There was an attempt to overthrow the king, not Louis XIV but another one. This person shot him, but did not kill him. The king recovered, the overthrow failed, and the shooter was drawn and quartered in the public square. I won't go into graphic detail, but drawn and quartered involves being torn apart in pieces.

This rule is the opposite of the last rule. If you are going to completely annihilate the other side, make sure they have no life left in them and no chance to stop the completion of the sale. Otherwise, they will get back at you somehow.

Basically, stay away from anyone who wants to destroy the other side. It is not good business and a miserable way to live. So, let's hope you never have to consider this rule.

11. Watch Out for "Group Think"

Irving Janus, a psychologist at Yale, coined the term "group think" to explain what happens to people when they are involved in a cohesive group: Their desire to be part of a unanimous group overrides the ability to look for alternative courses of action. Finding an alternative route frequently puts the deal together, and group think prevents the creativity necessary to find other solutions. Get the "group" to listen to you as the professional, instead of their well-meaning relatives or friends.

> *I represented an extended family in buying homes for several family members. They would bring all the members of the family, including all the children, to look at the homes that made "the short list." Then they would discuss how to proceed. By the time the discussion reached a conclusion, they had become determined that there would be only*

*one way to reach a successful conclusion to the ne-
gotiations. There were certain members of the family
that they listened to more than me. As a result, we
made offers on many, many homes before we were
successful in buying one. As a result, I don't work
with them anymore, as I have plenty of clients who
listen to my advice.*

12. Don't Let Your Clients Do Something Really Stupid

You need to have a graceful way to stop your clients from doing something really stupid. I have not found a way to confront
them directly without having that discussion ruin the relationship, so I use a story about another client, Sonya, and they get
the point. I helped Sonya sell and buy several properties, and
she was a very tough negotiator. At one point, she was going
to cancel an entire transaction because the buyer could not
get a written verification to us on the evening it was due. We
would have it in writing the next morning, and I had verbal
verification already. Sonya was under a lot of stress at work,
as she is a high-level executive. After a lot of discussion, she
finally said, "But you wouldn't let me do anything really stupid,
would you?" That became my rallying cry, and I told her she
could not call off the deal, as it was really stupid. Then I offered
to pay her anything she lost if I was wrong in saying she would
have this item in the morning. When I put my money where
my mouth is, she decided it was wise to wait until morning.
The verification came through, the sale closed, Sonya got a
great deal, and I got a good story.

Find a story from your own experience where you pre-
vented another client from doing something really stupid.

*For example, Chris Laurence, a real estate
agent from Front Royal, Virginia says, "I had a buyer
of a five-acre lot, several years ago. The asking price
was $50,000; we offered less, and after a couple of*

verbal counter offers, the seller was stuck at $49,000, while the buyer was stuck at $48,000.

The buyers loved the lot, as it had everything they wanted, but he was very stubborn and "on principle" refused to pay within $1,000 of the asking price. I said to him, 'In a couple of years time, when you are sitting on your deck admiring that view in your half-million dollar home, will you really care whether you paid $48,000 or $49,000 for the lot?' He got the point, agreed that he was being stupid, and the contract was ratified at $49,000. Later his wife told me, 'I also told him that if we lost it over $1,000, I would divorce him!'"

If you do not have a story from your own experience, you can refer to my rule that part of your job is to stop your clients from doing something really stupid, then launch into one of my stories by saying "I have a friend who...."

13. Try One More Time

Before you give up, try one more time, because sometimes one last effort gets the job done. It is called second effort in sports like football. If you have a stalemate, where the deal is going nowhere, give your counterpart the impression that you are giving up. That gesture takes the pressure off, as they think it is over. Then, ask your counterpart for some education that you can take out of the experience, so that you will do better next time. Say something like, "I must have presented this improperly to get this reaction." Typically, the counterpart will say, "No, there was nothing wrong with the presentation, the problem is ...." Listen very carefully to what the problem is, as you will be getting some unvarnished truth about the issue. This technique gives you one more chance to overcome what the problem is, and you may be able to snatch victory from the jaws of defeat.

Another version of trying one more time comes from Columbo, the television detective, who was always forgetting one thing that he had to ask. If you have not heard from your counterpart in such a long time that you think the negotiations are over, think of one more thing that you forgot to ask. "Did I give you a copy of the restrictions on the property, as you had asked for them? I can't see where I sent them." You are looking for anything to give you an excuse to call, but make sure it not such a dumb excuse that it shows you are too eager. If you just call to see what has happened to your offer, you will lose your negotiating position, but if you are following up on a minor point, you're calling to be professional. Then listen to them volunteer what the problem is. You get one more chance to solve the problem.

On occasion, it helps to change the cast of characters during the last effort. If there are personality clashes or big egos, see if you can bring in your manager or other respected third party.

> *One of the buyer's agents on my Team was representing a high-income client, and she showed him a particular property at his request. The listing agent claimed her buyer's agent was entitled to represent that client, as her buyer's agent had shown him the same property later. The listing agent would not take my calls. So I called her manager, who initially came on very strong due to misunderstanding the situation. She even tried to defend her agent not answering my calls, claiming that by attempting to discuss the situation I was harassing her agent. After several conversations, the manager helped my agent present an offer that was accepted on the property. The manager and I have a cordial relationship, and I get along with the other agent today.*

14. Be Nice

You will negotiate with the same group of real estate agents over and over. Be professional and be nice. You can disagree without being disagreeable. Many people do not mention "nice" and "Donald Trump" in the same breath, but his lawyer George Ross says in *Trump Style Negotiations* that "nice people are better negotiators and they get a higher percentage of satisfying outcomes." If even Trump aims to be nice, you can too.

If you are in a multiple offer bidding war with a number of other agents, the nice agent will get the property if their offer is anywhere close. You are known by the company you keep, and so are your clients. If you are a great person to work with, your counterpart will assume that your client is too. This can give you a competitive advantage, as well as the ability to get the benefit of the doubt when there are disputes.

One problem occurs when you are dealing with less-experienced agents. Some confuse kindness as a sign of weakness. If you have ever negotiated with lawyers, you watch out for the kind ones, as they are the ones strong enough that they do not have to show hostility to get their point across. When you test out whether kindness is weakness, you will find that the kind ones can politely dismantle you and your client. Experience will teach you that kindness is a sign of confidence and strength, but some inexperienced agents have not learned that yet.

Now that you know the rules, it is time for you to acquire the tools to create a great deal.

CHAPTER 9

TOOLS OF THE NEGOTIATING TRADE

There are certain tools in real estate negotiating that always work, because they give you ways to deal with common problems and perceptions. Unlike principles and rules, you can always use them, just choose the right tool for the situation. Also, these are not the "tricks," that is the next chapter. These are tools every well trained negotiator should be able to use.

1. Don't Pull Numbers From the Air

When you make an offer, or a counter offer, do you pick a round number? When the asking price is $1,400,000, do you offer $1,300,000? It looks like you pulled the number out of the air, I call it PFA for Pulled From Air.

Make yourself look more serious by picking something other than a round number. If you offered $1,321,755, it looks like you analyzed the situation in detail before making the offer. The number just appears to have more credibility to it. I am doing that now on a sale. The co-listing agent wanted to counter somewhere between $1,225,000 and $1,250,000. We chose $1,228,750 for the seller's counter offer, and the buyer increased their offer from $1,200,000 to accept it.

2. Make the Number Sound Better

If you are making an offer of $299,000 to buy a property, stretch a little farther and offer $300,000. The perception of the price makes it sound like so much more. Even better, couple this with the last rule and offer $300,455. If you are coming down from your selling price and were thinking of countering at $300,000, go down to $299,588 because it sounds like so much less. Marketing has been studying the perception of the price forever. Use it in your favor by making your buyer's offers appear higher and your seller's counter offers appear lower, so that your counterpart's reaction is better as you appear closer to agreement.

3. Take Smaller and Smaller Steps

With offers and counter offers, the two sides are moving closer on price. Start with your biggest change. Then, move less and less with each step. It takes the fun out of it for the other side and indicates that you are getting close to your limit.

Negotiation by Harvard Business Essentials makes the point that negotiating experts interpret a large concession as an indication that you have significant additional flexibility. So, if you give a large concession, your counterpart will think they can get additional significant concessions. Particularly in a buyer's market, it is important to get the buyer to want to continue the negotiations. In Los Angeles, buyers will occasionally make one offer and if they do not like the response, they will walk away, as their implicit needs are to show they are in control and demonstrate dominance. So, the large initial reduction makes it more likely the negotiations will continue, and the implicit needs of the buyer will be satisfied. The *Negotiation* book also makes the point that a small change generally signals that process is approaching the party's walk-away price, and that further efforts will result in smaller and smaller concessions.

If the seller is asking for $300,000 and the first offer is $275,000, you might come down $5,000 the first time, $3,000 the second time and $1,500 the last time when you also say you will not pay for the home warranty at that low price. When the buyer gets the feeling that they will only get a couple hundred dollars by going through one more round of negotiations, they are more likely to just accept your counter offer so they can wrap up the sale before another buyer appears.

4. Legitimacy

Most people defer to anything that appears legitimate, so you can use it to your advantage. Also, you need to know when this tool is being used on you, so you do not fall for it.

Examples are:

- Creating the image of legitimacy by the use of a pre-printed form, particularly if it says it was prepared by the state association of real estate agents after consultation with the atttorneys of the state bar association.
- Some builders get buyers to defer to their position and some real estate agents get their clients to accept their proposition by the appearance of legitimacy by saying that a particular point is "company policy."
- Create legitimacy by explaining how the position you are proposing meets the standards for an industry, such as showing that the way something was built complies with the building code.
- Creating legitimacy by getting an expert in the field to give an opinion supporting your position. When Martha Stewart used her position as an expert on home decorating to support the Twin

Lakes development in Cary, North Carolina, KB
Homes had more than three thousand people line
up for the first day of the grand opening.

The way to counter this tendency is to remember the
principle from the 1960s and question authority. I love Herb
Cohen's idea that the pre-printed form was not written by
"God's typewriter in the sky."

5. Deadlines

In *Trump Style Negotiation*, George Ross sites a study indicating 90 percent of the deals were made in the last 5 minutes before a deadline. Most people wait until a deadline
is looming before they reach an agreement. So, use this
tendency in your favor. Setting a deadline is particularly
important when you represent a buyer on a property that
is likely to have multiple offers because you want to get a
signed agreement before anyone else shows up.

Also, if you have something that is objectionable to
discuss, you might consider waiting until the deadline is
near and your counterpart is more likely to agree with your
request. Bring up an issue at the closing table, when your
counterpart has the goal in site, and you will more likely
get a concession. I am not fond of this use of the tool, as
you will also get a bad reputation with your counterparts
if you continually bring up problems at the closing table.
With collaborative negotiations, it is better to bring up the
issue early and maintain the cooperative relationship because you may need the relationship for any other issues
that arise. With win-lose negotiations, you do not have the
cooperation anyway, so push your counterpart up against
the deadline.

How do you pre-empt this move, if someone does it to
you? The counter to this move is to get a commitment that all
the issues are on the table well before the deadline.

I had so many agents from a particular realty company bring up problems at the closing table that were discovered at the walk through that I thought the firm was teaching this technique. To eliminate the problem, I do a pre-walk through before the buyers go through the house and take pictures of everything that is repaired to have proof that there is no problem with any repair issue. Then, I explain to them that if they do not call me at the walk through with a problem, I am not going to deal with it at the closing table. In other words, if they fail to give me the courtesy of a phone call to provide time to fix the problem before sitting at the closing table, they can pay for the repair out of their side of the commission as a way to apologize for their error in etiquette.

To counteract your counterpart's use of a deadline, if they try to impose one, test it. Find some reason to ask if you can have more time. If they are not firm, do not make concessions close to the deadline. The other use of your counterpart's deadline is to get your counterpart up against their own deadline, then ask for concessions.

Your clients can make this tool work to their detriment if they impose deadlines that are not absolutely necessary. Explain to your clients that any deadlines they impose on your side of the discussion will weaken their negotiating power because the deadline puts time pressure on you that your counterpart does not have. If there is a real need to buy the house before they leave town, fine. But, any unnecessary deadline is going to require your side to make more concessions than necessary.

6. Response to a Low Ball Offer

One important concept for any offer, including a low ball offer, is that any offer is an opportunity to put a sale together. So, every offer is good news. To counteract a client's emotional response to a low ball offer, I tell sellers the people they should be mad at are the ones who showed the house and did not bring an offer.

How you respond to an extremely low offer depends on the market. If it is even close to being a seller's market, thank the person for the offer and tell them you will be happy to respond when they want to get close to your price. Or, you can give them a counter offer at the full asking price, which is more likely to keep them in the game. My favorite response to this situation was one seller's agent who handed my client's low offer back to us saying "If the seller would consider that price, he would have asked for that price. Y'all come back when you are serious."

If the market is balanced, or favors the buyer, you may want to be kinder to the buyer. I like a "Courtesy Counter Offer." Come down ever so slightly, and indicate this was done just as a gesture to show you are interested in selling to this buyer. You do not want them to get the impression that you feel their first offer in any way sets an anchor or the tone for the negotiations. In this situation, be sure that you tell them you do not want to hear later on, "But I came up so much from my first offer." My response if I get that last statement is, "and if you had started at one dollar, you could have claimed to come up even more, but it still would have nothing to do with the value of the house."

The courtesy counter offer is an exception to the idea discussed above, where you come down the most at first, then decrease your changes in price. If the offer is way low, you do not want to signal that the buyer can get a big response to such a little effort on the buyer's part. Also, you do not want to signal that you will meet the buyer half way to his low ball price.

In *Trump Style Negotiation,* several of George Ross' examples indicate that he and Mr. Trump like to start with an outrageous proposal that they know has no chance of being accepted, then changing their style to agree with modifications to make the deal more palatable. This is a good illustration to use with your clients to calm them down after a "less than wonderful" offer, as you can explain that different people, and people from different backgrounds, negotiate differently, so they should not read too much of an insult into the proposal. It is just a matter of personal style.

7. Negotiating Seller Paid Closing Costs and Seller Paid Down Payments

Many buyers do not have enough cash for the downpayment and all of their costs, so they need the seller to pay the closing costs to make the deal work. Framing the negotiations in a manner favorable to your position makes a favorable result more likely. If you represent the seller, frame this idea by using net figures to make it more likely that both parties will accept the idea. If the buyer wants to offer $200,000 and needs $3,000 in closing costs, frame your discussions with your buyer that the net price is $200,000 and the $3,000 will need to be added to that price for a total offer of $203,000. Explain to the buyer that the house is being purchased for $200,000, and the buyer is also purchasing $3,000 worth of cash payments which costs the buyer $3,000. So, you negotiate with the net figure to agree on a price of $200,000, then add the closing costs to that price.

If you represent the buyer, frame it the opposite way. Have the discussions on price in terms of the total amount offered, including the closing costs, instead of discussing net figures. This makes it seem like you are offering more.

Net figures are even more important when you represent a seller responding to an offer. If your counter offer is in terms of a net price of $200,000 and you give the buyer the choice of adding as much closing costs as they need to that figure, it is more likely that their response will be higher, as they will be adding the funds they need to the net price.

Framing the price in this manner forces the buyer to look at what the seller is actually receiving, instead of the inflated price that has the closing costs built into it. I have had buyers tell me, "But we are giving the seller the asking price" when the total price was the asking price, and the seller was giving them back $5,000. That is not the asking price, it is $5,000 off the asking price.

Framing the negotiations in this manner also helps the seller's agent properly adjust the commission, by paying it on the net price, so that the seller does not have to pay a commission on the money that is immediately given back to the buyer. Having a seller pay a commission on money they do not get at closing makes for an unhappy seller. However, this practice varies throughout the United States, so paying the commission on the total price may be common in your area.

This same example works for situations where the buyer needs the seller to pay all or a portion of the down payment, like FHA loans through Nehemiah or Ameridream where the seller indirectly provides the down payment through a "donation" to a charitable organization and the charitable organization pays the buyer's closing costs. While this program has recently been ended, there are bills pending in Congress at the time of this writing to restore the program.

You need to be aware of the appraisal problems created by adding these costs to the price, particularly for the addition of the down payment. The house needs to appraise at the total price, not the net price, in order for the loan to fund. If there is an appraisal contingency, you may want to consider requiring the house to appraise for the net price, so that if the home does not appraise for the total price, the buyer will be more reasonable with any renegotiations required to get the sale to close.

I represented a family being relocated by IBM in a sale where we had an agreed price for a home of $197,000, with the seller paying $3,000 in closing *costs. The buyers did not need the seller to pay the closing costs, as they had enough money to close without the seller paid closing costs. However, it was more convenient for them to use that cash to fix up the house after closing instead of using it for closing costs. The appraisal was only $193,000. So, we gave the Seller two choices: (1) we could cancel the sale or (2) adjust the price to $193,000 and keep the sale.*

If the negotiations had been framed in terms of the net price, the agent for the seller would have immediately come back saying they might reduce the price, but they would not pay the closing costs at that lower price. Instead, the seller agreed to the lower price, and the buyers and I held our breath through the end of the closing, expecting that the seller would realize that he was giving us a house worth $193,000 for a price of $190,000 ($190,000 for the house and $3,000 for the closing costs). The seller signed everything and left the closing. After they were out of ear shot, the buyers cheered.

8. Negotiating with Builders

If you represent a builder selling homes, one of the best ways to negotiate is to have the image that you will not negotiate at all. In other words, get the other side to give up without trying. If you are a builder, you want the agents to look in the MLS and see that all of the homes in your neighborhood sold for the asking price with no discount off the price. Then, you hope the next agent may not even try to get a reduction in the price. When my Team represents a buyer, we always try to get something because they may have one property they really want to sell.

However, you will find that most builders will give you extra features in order to get their price. You give them their price, so they can maintain their image to the other real estate agents, but ask for additional hardwood flooring, better kitchen counter tops, upgraded appliances and buyer's closing costs.

> *Linda Soesbe, a real estate agent in Colorado Springs, Colorado, represented my daughter, Laurie Hughes, when she bought a home from a builder who said their prices would never be discounted in that neighborhood. Linda and I talked before they went into discuss the contract at the sales office and she had already thought of how to approach the builder. My daughter's house has a complete air conditioning system added to the property along with fully paid closing costs in return for the builder getting the asking price. When I visit in August, I appreciate the air conditioning.*

9. Commitment Before Closing

Some people are slippery when they are negotiating, as they keep bringing up other issues and nibbling to get a little more. When you are in this situation, get down to an identifiable number of issues that they want, preferably one. It is particularly important that you follow the principle of getting all the issues on the table at one time, preferably in a written document. Then, get a commitment that if you agree to that one issue, then they will agree to the entire deal. You do not use an open question, you use a closed question to get a commitment of yes or no.

For example, "Mr. Johnson, if I give you a quick closing date at the end of this month, then we will have a deal. Is that correct?" If Mr. Johnson says yes, change the closing date, get your buyer to initial it, and get it signed by Mr. Johnson, quickly. You want the commitment to stop the shifting position by Mr. Johnson, and you hold the possibility of a deal in front of his nose to get it.

10. Dealing with Bad Behavior

What do you do with a temper tantrum? There are several strategies, and one of the gentlest is to use "Feel, Felt, Found." Allow them to vent their feelings and wait for the emotion to subside, then show some empathy by saying "I understand how you feel. I have felt that way myself when (insert the name of the problem, but try to make it sound smaller than it is). But, after reflection I have found that (insert the other way of looking at the problem that you are trying to present)."

Ronald Shapiro and Mark Jankowski call their system E.A.R. in *Bullies, Tyrants and Impossible People*, which is an excellent book for learning how to deal with bad behavior. When you get an emotional outburst, start with Empathy to show that you understand their feelings. Be careful to show that you understand without giving the impression that you agree with their emotional demand. The next step is to Ask questions, mainly to give your counterpart time to calm down. While you are probing for information, you are encouraging them to get back to the issues with a phrase like "help me to understand..." so they can vent without feeling that they are being cross examined. The final step is to Reassure, without telling them what they need to do. A phrase like "I believe we can get this together" reassures, while "what you should do is" will only set them off again. Once you are back on the issues, your counterpart may be ripe for concessions as a way to apologize for the bad behavior, if the bad behavior is not just a ploy.

The most dangerous way to respond to an emotional outburst is to have one of your own. While it may be tempting, it usually escalates the emotions, removes the focus on the issues, and puts the transaction in jeopardy.

I use another technique if I am dealing with a professional real estate agent, as it does not work well with the truly overwrought. I start with "letting silence do the heavy lifting," so I do not react much other than to be quiet and watch. The person may feel better when they vent, and a little awkward at the silence. Then, I ask if this sort of behavior has worked for them in the past to get them what they want. I follow up by explaining that when I was a trial lawyer, my adversaries would throw tantrums when they had nothing else to support their position. So, I always took a tantrum to mean that the counterpart "was not holding any cards," i.e. had nothing. Then I ask if that is how I should interpret their behavior. With some people, shouting and threats are meant to get you off balance. By turning it around to show that you are taking it to mean that your counterpart is off balance, the behavior usually goes away. By the way, I rarely raise my voice and most of my team members have never heard me yell. If I do, duck.

What do you do with lying or bluffing? You need to know the normal behavior for the agents in your area, as bluffing is more acceptable in certain circles than in others. For example, in *Trump Style Negotiation*, George Ross gives a glimpse of what is appropriate in New York when he starts with the belief that every assumption he has about the information from his counterpart is wrong, then he is pleasantly surprised to find out some of it is right. That style of bluffing would not be well received in North Carolina. If you suspect bluffing, ask for independent validation. If your counterpart claims the house is larger than it is, offer to meet them at the house to measure it. If there is a claim that the house has had the plumbing replaced, ask for a receipt for the repairs or offer to look under the crawl space to be able to report back to your client. You can also ask for more detailed clarification, as most people cannot construct an extremely detailed lie without tripping over some detail. A third defense is to "walk away slowly," so that your counterpart has a chance to see that their bluff is a deal breaker, giving them the opportunity to call you back into the negotiations.

A lie ruins collaborative negotiations. Trust is an important element of collaborative negotiation. Finding out that your counterpart lied kills the trust, and there is no way to resurrect it.

Another thing you can do with lying or bluffing is to label everything represented as suspicious. This is close to saying to ignore everything they say. The only problem with this is that every now and then a liar tells the truth, which gets confusing. Otherwise, verify everything they say—for example, by requiring that all communications be in writing using email. You get a record of all the lies, which may be handy in the future. Or you may get a liar who is bright enough to stop lying since there is going to be a written record of everything that is said, thereby eliminating the problem.

Another approach is to see if you can bring in someone else, either on your side or on theirs. There may be a conflict of personalities that changing the players will cure. In essence, the best solution to dealing with a liar is to see if you can eliminate the liar and deal with someone else.

11. Use a Question to Respond

If you do not want to answer your counterpart, deflect their question with another question. In situations where revealing information would hurt your client and greatly help your counterpart, you may not want to reveal what you know, yet you do not want to lose your credibility. When you get in a tough spot, do not answer. Just ask a question. You do not need to change the subject, although it helps.

Another place a question can be a key tool is using it to get a commitment out of your counterpart. Some very successful real estate agents in Palos Verdes, California, used a great negotiating ploy by calling listing agents and asking about a property that was listed at $695,000. "Would they take $600,000 for the property?" If the agent answered yes, they will start negotiating below $600,000. Remember, the Code of Ethics for the National Association of real estate agents only lets you quote the listing price for the property. So, the proper response is "Are you offering me $600,000?" This technique is more important in face-to-face negotiations, so that you do not get a buyer who lowers your asking price then negotiates below that. With a proper question, the buyer makes a commitment to the price discussed, and you negotiate above that price.

12. Gradual Persuasion

You cannot eat an entire salami in one bite. You take it in little slices. If you want to reduce your listing's unreasonably high price, you may not be able to get it down in one step, but you may be able to reduce it in three steps.

One disadvantage of this three-step approach when applied to listings is that you will get a much better reaction from the market with one large price drop. The more dramatic drop gets a more dramatic reaction out of the buyers, because it completely repositions the property and they will worry that other buyers will jump on it. If you go down in small steps, and the market does not react—the buyers will not be worried that other buyers are going to go for it.

This concept applies when you are negotiating with a reluctant counterpart. In *The Weekend Millionaire Secrets to Negotiating Real Estate*, Roger Dawson and Mike Summey use the analogy of a small tug boat moving a supertanker. The tug boat does not do a full-speed run up and ram into the tanker; it gently engages the supertanker and pushes it a little at a time, gradually moving it to the desired position. If you can keep negotiations open, slowly making progress, you may be able to gradually move a difficult counterpart to an agreement. As long as the counterpart is still willing to listen, there is hope.

Decades ago, I had a relative who was in foreclosure, and the time to cure the default had passed before he let me know that there was a problem. In California foreclosures, there is a time in which you can just make the back payments on the loan, and it is reinstated. After that, you have to pay off the whole loan by getting new financing, and no bank wants to give a loan to someone who cannot make the payments on the old loan. We scheduled a meeting with a top-level member of the bank at his downtown office to discuss the possibility of a reinstatement. In today's climate, reinstatement is much more politically correct, with banks going the extra distance to avoid foreclosure. Decades ago, it was just another December day for the banker.

We kept talking about different options, different things we could do, and reasons why the bank would want to work with my family, as we had many members who had a long-term relationship with the bank (something that used to matter in days gone by). We were talking for over an hour, gradually changing the banker's position. The banker gradually appreciated that my relative was a nice guy with a family. Finally, his face brightened and he said, "All right, we will allow you to reinstate the loan if you can make the payment by tomorrow." I wrote him a check to reinstate it right there, and our family had a much better Christmas.

13. Translate Issues into Numbers: Small Numbers for One Result, Huge Numbers for Another Result

Many concessions are difficult for a client to consider in the abstract. Will the seller do a particular repair? Can the closing date be moved? Instead of hearing, "It is the principle of the thing" while your client digs in his heels, translate the problem into dollars and cents. Viewing it in terms of cold, hard cash will make more sense, as it takes the principle out of it. Then, negotiate the money.

Translate a problem into small numbers if you want to show how easy it is to accept a proposal. It may be difficult to convince a buyer to come up by $3,000 to close a sale on a $150,000 house, as it sounds like a big number. If the interest rates are low, the increase in the monthly payment on a $1,000 increase in the loan is under $6. So, the buyer can have the home they love if they can handle $18 per month. If they skip going out to lunch at an inexpensive restaurant once a month, they can live where they want. The image of giving up one lunch at Applebee's to get the home with the right schools for your children makes the decision easier.

Translate the problem into a huge number if you want the opposite result. If you have a seller who wants to rent back for two weeks and promises to be out right on time, you may want to translate the problem into a huge number to guarantee that they will be out. The rent for the two weeks may be at the buyer's holding costs (principle, interest, taxes, and insurance) to be reasonable, but any holdover after the two weeks will be at $10,000 per day. If the seller says, "It looks like you want to make it difficult for me to delay moving out past the agreed date," you can reply that actually you are trying to make it impossible to stay over. Margaret Rome, a real estate agent in Baltimore, taught me this technique to use when it is critical that you get performance on an issue that is important to your client. If the high figure is in the contract, you will not get a request from the seller to stay a little longer, as the issue has been translated into a dollar amount that makes it worth the effort to move on time.

14. Getting Past an Impasse

If you are stuck, change something: The terms, the price, the closing date, the time for inspections, the condition of the property—anything. See if you can work on anything else, get it resolved, then come back to the sticking point to see if the momentum of working out the other issue carries over to this issue. If you can brainstorm with your counterpart to create a series of choices that resolve the sticking point, you may be able to get one, or both, parties to be happy with that menu of options. Choosing one of the choices feels like being in control, so it may make that party feel victorious.

Another technique for moving past an impasse is to discuss problems "off the record" with your counterpart. If the discussions do not count, you might get some suggestions that will help you move your clients to an acceptable position.

If you are really stuck, the buyer can always change the house they want to buy, and the seller can change the buyer they want to sell to. In other words, walk away gracefully; the parties might come back. If they call you back, your negotiating power just increased.

15. Back Up Offers

If your client's favorite house already has a signed contract of sale, you should consider a back up offer. My Team does not show properties that have strong contracts on them, because there is no reason to get a buyer to fall in love with a home they cannot have. With their unrequited love, buyers in this situation will tell you that no other house compares favorably to the one that got away.

If you do need to try to get a house with a sales contract, a back up offer is an excellent tool that is under utilized. The back up offer is a formal contract that is accepted by the seller with a contingency that it becomes effective on the cancellation of the current contract. With a signed back up contract, your buyer avoids any competition that may occur if the current sale is cancelled and several interested buyers show up, because your back up contract specifies that your client gets the house with a specified price and terms immediately on the cancellation of the current contract. Also, your buyer can withdraw the back up offer at any time before the cancellation of the current contract. So, your client can keep looking at other homes and if a better one is found, your client can buy it.

In this manner the back up offer gives your client the best of both worlds. Your buyer controls who gets the house if the current sale is cancelled, but your buyer is not bound to buy the house until the current sale is cancelled.

If the terms of your back up offer are equal to the current offer, you give the seller the power to be strict with the current buyer, so that they can refuse to do inappropriate repairs with the confidence that your buyer will be waiting. In the event that your back up offer has better terms, you give the seller an incentive to get rid of the other buyer knowing that they will get a better deal with your client. So, do not ask the listing agent to call you if the other sale falls through, get control of the property with a back up offer and give the seller an incentive to get rid of the other buyer.

16. Use Humor

You can get much more done with laughter than you can with any other emotion. Calming a tense situation with a humorous response frequently gets agreement, as well as appreciation from all the parties, as it makes the process more fun. Don't take yourself too seriously, as humor is disarming.

You can avoid answering a tough question by joking, or make the answer more palatable with a joke.

A client of mine was asking for a concession on the "as is" clause required by the bank seller, as he wanted some improvement in the condition of the house. With a big smile, the banker said, "We could also see if I could get my wife to come clean the house once a week." When the laughter subsided, my client said he understood the bank's position.

With decades of experience as a real estate agent, Dianne Dunn of New Bern, North Carolina, has an illustration of how to use humor to get a wonderful result from an attempt by a client to cut her commission. She relates, "I had a seller recently receive an offer within five days of listing the home for sale, in a market where the absorption rate is eight months. When the sellers asked me how much of a 'discount' I was going to give them for such a short time on the market, I smiled and said 'Discount? Actually, I was thinking more in terms of a bonus for such a quick sale!' The sellers laughed, and the commission did not change."

With these tools in your toolbox, you will be much more successful in creating great deals. The next chapter has all the tricks that you will wish you had known before they were used on you.

CHAPTER 10

TECHNIQUES AND TRICKS

Most people want me to teach them the "tricks and gambits." Frankly, understanding the structure of negotiations, having certain principles, following your rules, being able to use the right tools and doing the research to give yourself the most knowledge possible will be more important in your results than some clever maneuver. Some of them are useful ones that you will employ and they are fun to know.

It is also important to be able to recognize some of these techniques when your counterpart is using them so that you can point out your recognition of the trick to your counterpart. There are two predominant ways to do this (1) express your feelings because no one can dispute your feelings or (2) use humor so you do not get bogged down in analyzing the maneuver. Doing this typically ends with getting back on track with the negotiations.

Here are some of my favorites:

1. Split the Difference

I went to a Continuing Legal Education seminar that taught attorneys to negotiate, since I am required to take this type of course as an Attorney. The instructor handed out a particular fact situation to everyone in attendance, described on a couple of pages so it was always the same facts, presented in the same way. Everyone in the room divided up into pairs. He asked the attorney on the left to represent one side, the attorney on the right to represent the other side and told them to negotiate toward a settlement. He asked everyone to keep track of certain things, such as where they each started with the financial offer, and where they ended up. He had run this same situation over one thousand times. He found that the vast majority of negotiations ended in a settlement that was close to half way between where each side started. Some negotiations did not reach a settlement, but when they did, a huge number settled nearly half way between each starting point. In other words, most of the time, the parties split the difference between their starting positions.

This technique is frequently used to finish negotiations, if you have been going back and forth several times. Tell the other agent that you can keep going back and forth more and more, but you are going to end up in the middle. "So let's make each one of our clients equally unhappy, and meet in the middle." This move is a particularly wise if you represent the buyer, as the buyer needs to finish the negotiations quickly and get a signed contract before some other buyer shows up to make a competing offer on the house. Remember, your primary goal is to buy the house, so missing the purchase by going around too many times lets your secondary goal of getting a better price defeat your primary goal of buying the house.

Do not do this as the first move in negotiations. If your asking price is $600,000 and the buyer offers $550,000, do not go through the same meet in the middle approach right away. Logically, it should be the same, as you know you are going to end up in the middle. But, buying a house is emotional, not logical. So, let the negotiations progress naturally. I explain it to my clients that "some people like to waltz, so you need to let them enjoy the dance." "Split the difference" works when the participants are tiring of the process. When I was a solo agent, without a team, selling a good number of homes, I experimented on many occasions with "getting down to it" and trying to meet in the middle as the first response by a seller, particularly for sellers with Marston's director personality (D) that like to finish negotiations quickly. It worked once. Every other time, the buyer wanted to try us out again, frequently adopting our logic and proposing to split the difference again. In other words, they wanted us to meet them half way from our counter offer to their original offer. When it works only once out of all the times I tried, it does not work. Don't do it too early, because it nearly always fails.

The other lesson to learn from my failed experiments of splitting the difference is to get the other person to offer to split the difference. If they offer, and you accept reluctantly, they feel like they won. If you offer to split the difference, and they are forced to accept, they do not get that feeling of victory.

Once you know this tendency in negotiating, you can work backwards to predict what someone will settle for. If a buyer makes you an offer of $550,000 on your asking price of $600,000, they are signaling that they will pay $575,000 if you are just an average negotiator. If you will settle for that, just get started. If you want $580,000, you need to design a game plan to get more out of the buyer.

You can also use this idea in establishing your opening proposal after figuring out where you want to end up, by bracketing your final result. If you want to end up at $550,000 on a property that is asking $600,000, start with an offer of $500,000. Then, as the other side moves down, move up in a similar amount to their change in position, so that you keep your final result in the middle of the difference between the negotiating positions. You will have to vary your counter offers somewhat, because if they are too predictable, it will be too obvious to your counterpart what you are doing. But, if you start twice as far away from their asking price as where you want to be, when you come up by half that amount, you will be at your desired result.

While splitting the difference may have a ring of fairness since each party is giving up the same amount at that time, it is not necessarily logical. If the buyer has started from an extremely low price relative to the true value of the property, offering to split the difference will give a result that is not fair for the seller. Similarly, if the seller has been coming down less than the buyer has been coming up, splitting the difference would give a result that is not advantageous to the buyer. Be aware that what sounds like a fair concept can give unfair results, because you may not end up at a value that reflects the market value of the property.

2. Package Option

When I was younger, many menus in Chinese restaurants let you pick one item from column A or one item from column B. The more technical term for this is a Package Option. This technique for counter offers is to give your counterpart a choice, i.e. a two pronged counter offer. You can have a price of $210,000 with the playhouse, washer, dryer and refrigerator or $208,000 without those items. The benefit of this type of counter offer is that the counterpart frequently picks one, as they are so busy concentrating on the two choices that they do not think of the fact that they can choose neither one and make another counter offer. Another benefit is that the counterpart does not feel like they are being pushed into a corner by being forced to take one option, as they have two (or more) options, and they have the last word.

Be aware that there is a frequent response to this type of offer. The counterpart will take the best of both choices. In the example, it is not unusual for the counterpart to come back saying they want the price of $208,000 with the sale including the playhouse, washer, dryer and refrigerator. So, if you are looking to close negotiations, give your counterpart a Package Option, but be sure you will be happy if they take

the best of both choices. Either way, you will finish the negotiations, whether they accept one of the choices, or propose
the best of both choices.

If you are dealing with a inexperienced or rigid real
estate agent, this choice can confuse them. So, evaluate
whether your counterpart is intelligent enough to handle
the choices that this technique provides.

You can use this technique when you want to get any
decision. When you are negotiating to set an appointment,
instead of asking, "When do you want me to come over to
list your house?" ask "Would tonight be good or tomorrow be
better?" They will frequently pick one of the two, instead
of thinking that one of their other choices is to not set the
appointment at all.

3. Set Aside

If you hit a sticking point, try setting that issue aside until
later. If you get agreement on the other issues, the momentum of reaching agreement on the other points sometimes
carries over to the issue that you set aside, so it gets resolved
more easily. The other factor that comes into play is that the
participants have invested more time and effort in reaching a
deal, so the more time invested the more likely it is that they
will try harder to succeed on this last point.

Some novice negotiators think that it is best to tackle
the major issues first, and stay with them until they are
resolved. Frequently, it is better to establish a rapport by
getting a number of agreements, then use the good will it
has created to get more flexibility on the issue that has
caused the impasse.

4. Nibble

I learned this one from Law and Motion hearings in court
when I was a trial lawyer. I noticed that when the judge was

about to finish making a ruling, just at the end of the judge's statement, one of the attorneys would ask for something and make it sound like a clarification. "Your Honor, of course that ruling includes...." They were actually asking for just one more little item. So, I learned to grab for that last little item at the last moment before the gavel came down by presenting it as though it was an understood part of the process and I am just verifying that the item is included in the decision.

Then I read Herb Cohen's classic book, *You Can Negotiate Anything,* and found out it was called a nibble. This technique works best when you are finalizing negotiations either in person or over the phone, but not so well in email or written offers, as you are trying to catch the other side with an agreement nearly in their grasp. You have to seize the moment and get the last item while they are in the process of agreeing. You get them to throw in one more little thing under the guise of clarifying that this item was included all along. So, your buyer is just about to sign the contract with a builder at their sales office, when you say "of course, this includes stainless steel appliances." The builder wants to get the deal done and throws in the stainless steel appliances.

Why does this work? Before coming to an agreement, your counterpart is resisting the proposal. After reaching an agreement, most people want to believe what they have done is to make a good decision. So, they want to support that decision and not have to re-open negotiations. If all they have to do is throw in one more thing they are more likely to do it now that they are in a position of supporting the agreement. On occasion, you can gently revisit issues that your counterpart previously rejected at the last minute before the papers are signed, as your counterpart is more vulnerable at that time because of this shift from resisting the agreement to supporting the agreement.

How do you defend against a nibble? The easiest way is to ask for something in return when your counterpart asks for something. In the example, the builder would put a price on the stainless steel appliances. Another defense is to call it what it is, but doing it in a friendly manner. When your counterpart asks for the refrigerator in addition to the washer and dryer just as they are about to sign the acceptance, remind them that they got a great deal already so they do not want to jeopardize the sale by re-opening all the terms of the negotiations. You want to make them feel as if they are reneging on a commitment, but you have to do it gently, and a smile helps.

Humor is another good way to defend against a nibble. If you cannot think of something funny, a smile may be enough.

5. Flinch and Vise

The flinch is also called the wince. Your counterpart proposes something, and you grimace, that is the flinch. My favorite phrase to express the vise is "You'll have to do better than that." They are similar techniques. If someone makes a proposal, and you want to improve it right away, say "You will have to do better than that" with a wince on your face. If the proposal was a trial balloon, where the proponent was looking for a reaction, you will frequently get a better proposal. If you cannot get a better proposal, you have discovered that your counterpart cannot do any better.

This technique can be applied when you are the agent for a buyer who wants to propose a low ball offer. When they suggest it in your office, you wince, and they propose a more reasonable offer. This will avoid some damage to the negotiating process, as starting too low is insulting in some circles. Some people believe that the lower you start, the better the price you will get, which is true if all the parties accept the first offer as a legitimate anchor for the negotiations. However, in the Triangle area of North Carolina, if you insult a southern family with a low ball offer, they will make you apologize financially by selling the home to you at a much higher price than they would have if you had treated them with respect, if they will sell it to you at all. This is true for many sellers throughout the United States. So, by flinching, you are helping your client avoid this result.

A gentler way to accomplish the vise is to suggest to your counterpart that opening negotiations with the offer they propose may make your client angry. Let your counterpart know that you are happy to present the offer as it is, but share your fear that it will set your client off. You can suggest that they may want to reconsider, as an angry seller usually makes that buyer pay more in the long run. Using a tone of working together with the other agent works much better than insulting the quality of the offer being presented.

To reverse this concept, you can use the "Shock and Awe" technique of calling up a listing agent and proposing an extremely low offer. If you do not get a flinch reaction, you might try it. Even if you do get the flinch and you start with a better offer, your concession of increasing the price has some perceived value to the listing agent, and hopefully that value gets communicated to their client.

One of the simplest ways to flinch is to ask, "Is that your best offer?" It gives your counterpart a chance to improve their offer, without you having to counter their offer. Frankly, you should practice, "Is that the best you can do?" with nearly every purchase.

The best way to respond to this technique is with a question, like "Just how much better do you need?" Ask it in a friendly tone, so you do not react to the apparent shock of the other party that is part of the vise performance. Don't change your proposal just because of a flinch or vise, but you may want to get your counterpart to respond with their own proposal by asking a good question. Another way to counter the flinch or vise is to say nothing and "let silence do the heavy lifting." A third response is to flinch back, and give the same reaction to the other party. A fourth response is to repeat your offer, showing you believe it is reasonable. A fifth response is to "walk away slowly" indicating that since the positions are so far apart, there is no need to continue. If they let you walk, the wince was real. If they bring you back, it wasn't.

Keep in mind that you do not want to bid against yourself when you react to a flinch or a vise. Get the counterpart to give you a counter offer before you increase your offer, unless you think the advice to avoid angering the seller is accurate.

6. Higher Authority & Good Cop, Bad Cop

The builder's agent in the sales office has to get the contract approved by the main office, a negotiating technique called "Higher Authority". This technique is the same one used by most car dealerships. This gives the higher authority the ability to either nibble, or come back with a counter offer. Meanwhile, the onsite agent gets to say their hands are tied. To counter this technique, start to Walk Away Slowly by beginning to leave the sales office. You will quickly find out whether the agent's hands are tied or not, as most of them will try to keep you from walking away by letting you know just how far the main office will go.

Another way to deal with this is to find out what the sales agent can do without corporate authorization, so you can get as much as possible without playing the game. The next best thing is to find out what the onsite agent can recommend to the main office. It is better to have these discussions before your client arrives, so they can be done privately when the onsite agent is more likely to talk freely. If you can get the onsite agent on your side, you will get the classic "good cop, bad cop" situation, where the onsite agent is trying to persuade the unseen higher authority.

The reason that builders and others use higher authority is it makes you give them a better proposal, as you not only have to convince the person in front of you, you have to give them enough to work with so that they can convince the higher authority. Also, it puts you in a position of needing to get the onsite agent on your side to persuade the higher authority, so you will do more for them. With this technique, the onsite agent can use trial balloons that they do not have to stand behind to get you to alter your position, such as, "If you can come up another $5,000, I would have a better chance at getting this approved." Once it goes to the "main office," the reply can be to use the vise technique of telling you, "You will have to do better than that," even after you came up by the $5,000. Furthermore, this tool allows the onsite agent to use the auction effect by implying that there are others interested in this property, so there may be competing offers being reviewed by the head office.

If you are dealing with an individual buyer you need to find out if they are going to use the higher authority technique of checking with someone else before they make a decision. The way to eliminate this tactic is to ask a Howard Brinton type question, such as, "If we find a great house for you today, is there any reason why you cannot make an offer?" I like to follow that one up with "Did you bring your checkbook?" Once you have established that there is no higher authority, you will not get the "we need to ask Uncle Harry what he thinks" statement.

Similarly, the defense to the higher authority maneuver is to find out the decision making process before you start. If the counterpart says there is a higher authority who must approve the deal, see if you can meet with that authority for the real negotiations.

I lost a good client, as well as a buyer's agent, when a bank wanted to keep their higher authority gambit in place after we had set up a meeting at their offices with assurances from their agent that all decision makers would be at the table. When the bank officer would not let the buyer, a prominent attorney, negotiate directly with the decision maker on a property in Lunada Pointe in Rancho Palos Verdes,

California, he walked out and bought another house. After many more months on the market, the bank ultimately sold the foreclosed house for considerably less than what this buyer was prepared to offer. This is one of the reasons I prefer to structure negotiations where all interested parties come together, as playing games sometimes loses everything.

If you do get an objection that the proposal needs to be reviewed by a higher authority, see if you can narrow the review. Then, write up an offer, or a contract, with a condition that it be reviewed for a limited purpose within a limited time. I put conditions in my Short Sale contracts (a sale where there is not enough money to pay the loans on the property) that the seller have it reviewed by a tax professional within 10 days to see if the sale qualifies for the new legislation that eliminates income tax to the seller on the amount that is not repaid to the bank. The seller has accepted the transaction, and the only review will be for tax purposes within ten days.

Another way to counter the higher authority is to "divide and conquer." Tell the "good cop" that you can't agree to the concession requested, and since the "good cop" empathizes with your position, say that the "good cop" will have to persuade the "bad cop". Since the "good cop" agrees with (or at least understands) your position, you ask him if he can recommend it to the "bad cop." A different way to divide and conquer is to tell the good cop that it looks like the bad cop is too upset to continue the negotiations, so offer to come back at a better time. This may get the bad cop performance to end.

If your proposal has to be reviewed by the higher authority, get a commitment from the person you are dealing with that they will recommend the proposal to the higher authority, so that the status of your contact person is in play. Another way to accomplish the ego involvement of your counterpart is to ask if the higher authority generally approves their efforts.

7. The Decoy

This is also called the Red Herring, for a trick that was used in fox hunts in England. The story goes that a smelly herring would be dragged across the trail of the fox to try to divert the hounds.

In short, you put an issue into the negotiations that you really do not care about. Get your counterpart to follow your smelly fish bait by building up the item so that your counterpart thinks it is something important. In this manner, if you concede it, the counterpart feels a great victory. A variation of this concept is to put an issue on the table that you know your counterpart cannot agree to, so that it is important for them to get you to concede. You ask for a quick closing on a home where the sellers want to wait a normal amount of time so their children can finish the school year. You know they will not agree to the quick closing, but you build it up by pointing out what it will mean to you to be able to move in quickly. When the sellers cannot go for the quick closing, you ask for a much better price in return for letting them dictate the date of the closing.

> *Margaret Rome, a real estate agent from Baltimore, Maryland, had a home her clients loved, but could not afford unless they got a great price. The sellers were particularly proud of two new white couches and other decorations in their living room. The buyers couldn't care less about the couches, but Margaret wrote up an offer asking for the house at a low price, and included the couches and other furniture in the purchase. The sellers spent a great deal of time in their counter offer justifying the elimination*

of the furniture from the negotiations, and came down enough on the price that the buyers could afford the property.

The counter measure to the decoy is to ask your counterpart to explain in great detail why the issue is so important. When the explanation stumbles, you know it is a decoy. Similarly, you can ask where this issue stands in the hierarchy of issues and ask what they will concede if you give in on that issue. When they show little value for that item, it is a decoy. Probably the best response is to use the "set aside" by going on to other issues. Once you resolve all the other issues, the decoy will disappear.

9. Ultimatum: Take It or Leave It

If you get to the absolute bottom line, say so. If you do not want to negotiate any more, say so. This is the way to signal that you have been pushed to your limit. But, be ready for this message to end negotiations. Don't say it is your final offer, then return to the negotiations because you will look like you are dishonest and playing games. If you have to come back again, you need a good reason for why something changed, such as you can get a better loan now so you can afford more.

A better way to present this in collaborative negotiations is to say "This is the best I can do." "Take it or leave it" is an aggressive way to say that you will be breaking off the negotiations if the point is not accepted. This alternative does not say you are ending the negotiations while it indicates you are at your bottom line.

There are several defenses to an ultimatum. My favorite is to continue as if it was not given, that this is just another negotiating posture. Another is to test the ultimatum by acknowledging that this is the end of the negotiations so you walk away slowly. When your counterpart sees everything coming apart, their position frequently softens. Another retort is to test the maneuver by asking what would happen if you could come up with an even better proposal than the "take it or leave it" proposition. If the response shows interest, then it is not really the bottom line for the negotiations. You can also take the ultimatum apart by asking which part of the proposal is final, so that there may be further negotiations on other terms. Then, propose a change in those other terms for a change in the "take it or leave it" issue. Another option is to take their position with a condition that they accept one final change on your part, so you use a "nibble."

If you decide to "leave it", leave gracefully. You want to leave the door open to further negotiations. If your counterpart comes back to you after you have gracefully rejected their ultimatum, you are in a much stronger position because they have signaled that they need you more than you need them.

Most people use this technique as a bluff, so I rarely believe this presentation. If I had a dollar for every time I have heard that this was the final offer, when it was not, I could afford to give this book to every real estate agent in the United States.

10. The Reverse Offer

Normal procedure is for a seller to wait for a buyer to make them an offer, just like it was proper etiquette for a young lady to wait for a gentleman to ask her to dance. In the same manner that modern ladies are asking men to dance, a seller can make an offer to a buyer to start negotiations in a technique called a reverse offer.

The agent for the seller proposes an offer to the buyer for the sale of the house that has better price or terms than what is offered in the Multiple Listing Service, so there is a special benefit to the offer. Then, the listing agent has to create a sense of urgency by putting a time limit on the proposal, so that the benefit disappears when the time limit passes.

Since written offers are much more likely to get serious consideration, you may want to put the seller's proposal in writing and have it signed. Check with your broker in charge before you do this, because you will have an offer on the table that the buyer can accept any time before the specified time limit. If another offer comes in, you may be in a position of having to formally revoke the reverse offer before it is accepted. A problem may arise if the reverse offer is signed and the acceptance communicated before your revocation is documented. However, in a buyer's market where there are few offers the odds of this happening are small, and the possible result is not so horrible as you have a contract with terms that your seller actually proposed.

Since this offer is contrary to long standing conventions, you may need to take some time explaining it to a buyer's agent who has never seen it before. Make that agent feel special, as you are taking the time to give them an offer that can be used to put a deal together, while no other seller is going to that effort.

The downside of this procedure is that the seller looks extremely eager to make a deal, so the buyer frequently counters with an offer that is worse. However, this downside is appealing in a slow market, as you have at least started negotiations.

Try out these techniques in unimportant situations so you can practice when the results do not count much. When the seller at the farmer's market gives you a price for corn, try the flinch. These maneuvers are useful, but you have to practice them to make them work smoothly. Trying one for the first time in an important negotiation will let you learn how to use it, but you will wish you had practiced a few times before.

Now you know the techniques and maneuvers, you should learn what to do when there are multiple offers on a property.

There can be times when a property receives a flurry of offers. If there is more than one offer on a property, the techniques of negotiating change completely. It is amazing how much more a buyer wants a property when it is discovered that someone else wants it.

Knowing how to work in a multiple offers situation is one of the most valuable negotiating talents a real estate agent can have. When you represent a buyer, you can make the difference between their children growing up in the home they love or not. For sellers, you can get a sale that closes for sure, frequently with an amazing price.

What's the best way to get either a better sale for your seller or increase the chances of success for your buyer? As usual, the procedures are completely different if you represent the buyer or the seller, so let's start with the procedure for the seller.

When the Seller Receives Multiple Offers

You want to create competition for the property. So, you want to consider all the offers at the same time. You need to force anyone who is interested in the property to cooperate with your game plan of reviewing offers at a certain time. To do this, you set a deadline for all the buyers to make their offers and state that you will respond at a certain time. Just like an auction or a one-day sale at a department store, the urgency gets action and more sales.

The better buyer's agents will want to know what factors are important to the sellers, other than price—such as the closing date, what kind of proof is needed to show that the buyer can obtain financing, what sort of verification the seller will accept that the buyer has the down payment available, and what else is important to the seller. The buyer's agents want to know everything that will improve their offer in the eyes of the seller. It is in your seller's best interest that you guide the buyers to a proposal that has everything the seller wants.

How to respond to multiple offers

Some agents will pick one buyer from all the suitors and negotiate with that one first. I disagree with this method because it does not create an auction effect, in which the buyers bid higher. It is also flawed because all the buyers who did not get a chance will complain that their offers were not properly considered, so you will have a difficult time getting the same agents to show your other listings that have the potential for multiple offers. As a real estate agent, you need to give everyone who works hard to sell your listings a fair chance. Otherwise, it hurts your relationship with the real estate community.

Some listing agents will provide the same counter offer to all the suitors specifying the terms they will accept. This is not the best choice on the issue of price, but it is a good idea when you are dealing with all the other terms of the sale. If you specify the price in your counter offer, the seller will get a lower price because you have put an anchor in the negotiations: the buyers will react to your proposed price and use it as an upper limit on what they will offer. .

My technique is to provide a counter offer to each suitor

that corrects the unacceptable terms in each offer—that is, change everything to terms that the seller will accept, but leave out any reaction to the price. Then ask each suitor to give their "last, best, and final offer" on price so that every suitor will have to worry about what every other bidder is doing. This will make them aim higher than they would have if you had specified a price—and most likely higher than your seller would have asked, due to the auction effect. Also it has the advantage of giving every buyer an equal chance to get the house, so you do not get complaints from the buyers who lost.

You have to comply with the provisions of the National Association of REALTORS® Code of Ethics requirement that all offers be presented to the seller promptly. You present them promptly, then you set a time at which your seller will respond. If it is beyond the time limit set by that buyer in their offer, give that buyer the opportunity to extend their time limit, If the buyer will not consent to change the time for the seller's response, you have to discuss the options with the seller to either (1) deal with this offer now, particularly if it is exceptionally good, or (2) thank the buyer for the offer but say that you are not going to respond within the time requested; in other words, you reject their offer and proceed with the other interested parties. In all of this, you must be sure your procedure complies with the local rules of ethics.

Selecting the best buyer

You have to pick the best buyer, not just the highest bid. When you evaluate the offers, the most important features are (1) the ability to close the sale and (2) the quality of proof that the buyer has the cash to purchase the house (in a cash sale) or that the buyer has the down payment and the financing available in a conventional sale. Most people concentrate on the price. Instead, you should concentrate on the buyer's ability to close—that is, to make it all the way through the process to a successful completion of the sale. Why is this important?

There are few experiences more humbling than selecting a buyer with the highest price only to have it turn out that you picked someone who cannot close the sale. You will quickly find that the negotiating dynamics are ruined and that you will have moved very quickly from a position of power to an extremely weak position. Some of the buyers will have purchased other homes, and begging the rest of them to come back will change you from being sought after to being the one doing the chasing.

At this point, you also have to put the home back on the market. Living through this just once will teach you never to select a marginal buyer again. The only way to get multiple offers is to create competition and urgency. Putting a home back on the market after a sale falls through, with all the real estate agents wondering what is wrong with it, is not the right setting for getting multiple offers again.

How to represent a seller: A Case Study

My Team represented a long-term client selling his Rancho Palos Verdes home in 2003, when the market was starting to get very hot for sellers. The comparable sales indicated the home should be worth $850,000, so we intentionally underpriced it at $825,000 after discussing our game plan with our client. We wanted to get an auction effect going, and underpricing it would get everyone's attention. To add to the auction effect, the client was a professional poker player who worked nights and slept until early afternoon, so we only allowed the home to be shown between 2 p.m and dark. We made it known that offers would be considered at the end of a week. There were buyers swarming over each other to get to the home during the limited hours, which meant that every buyer could see that there were other buyers interested in the property. As a result, the sense of urgency for the property was huge.

We had eight top-quality offers to consider. We could have had many more, as we told a number of agents that their situation would put them in a lower category even though we would be happy to present their offer. We created an Excel spreadsheet to compare the important qualities found in each offer. We went back to everyone who made an offer with a letter from me listing the factors that were important to the seller, with minimum standards on certain things, such as the closing date. The unsigned letter from me as the real estate agent gave none of the buyers an opportunity to claim that they could sign anything and create a binding contract because it clearly stated it was not a counter offer from the seller but suggestions from his real estate agent on terms that the seller would favor. The letter asked the buyers for their "last, best, and final" offer, stating everyone would have one chance to impress the seller. Now, California has a good multiple counter offer form, but it was not available then.

We told the agents in writing that no one could come back after the specified time to improve their offer, so they should not hold anything back. What we DIDN'T tell them was that we were selecting buyers based on their ability to close, with the second factor being the price they offered. This meant that the highly qualified buyers focused on price.

One buyer came in with a copy of a bank statement showing they had the down payment, closing costs, and even more money in the bank. They submitted a full loan approval, not a pre-qualification or pre-approval letter, as they had gone completely through loan underwriting. The down payment was more than 30 percent. The buyer waived the appraisal contingency, so that if the house did not appraise high enough to get the financing specified in the contract, they would put in more money for the down payment. Furthermore, their bank statements proved that they had the additional funds to complete the sale, if the appraisal was not high enough. As the finishing touch, they specified that they would offer $5,000 higher than any other legitimate offer in an escalation clause. They were represented by an agent whom I had known for decades, so I could trust everything she represented. We had a winner.

My Team received thank-you notes from a couple of buyers who lost, as they felt they had been given a fair chance to get the home. The home sold well over our estimate of the market value and closed right on time.

Expect the buyer's revenge

You push the buyers to the limit. At some point, they are going to push back. So, you need to expect that the buyers are going to ask for something special before they close. Since they have been forced to go through an invasive procedure for their offer, endure a bidding war and bid the top price, at some point during the contract period the buyers will ask for something in return. Normally, it is something to do with the condition of the house, which is logical because they paid top dollar so they expect that the house will be in excellent condition.

You need to prepare your seller for this reaction. If it comes as a surprise, the seller will over react, saying that the repairs should not be done because there was so much interest in this house. However, the interest was at the time of the bidding war, and that time has past. If the seller expects the revenge is going to happen, it is just part of your game plan and the repair discussions are much easier.

In the example above, the buyers wanted lots of little things to be improved or repaired. Since we had plenty of money coming from the sale, we could easily persuade the seller to do all the requested repairs.

If you want to try to counteract this effect, you can ask the buyers to purchase the property "as is". In a raging seller's market, you can get away with that. However, many agents cannot handle an "as is" discussion and most buyers do not honor the "as is" clause so they ask for repairs anyway, as we discuss in Chapter 12. You can try to counteract this buyer's revenge, but set your seller's expectations that they are going to give something to the buyer before closing. If the buyer is one of the rare ones who does not ask for anything, your seller will enjoy it more.

Buyer's Procedure for Multiple Offers

When you represent the buyer, your objective is to be the successful bidder, but you have to follow Rule 12 in Chapter 8, Don't Let Your Client do Anything Really Stupid. The first thing you need to discuss with your client is how badly they want the home. Some buyers will not participate in a bidding war, in which case you move on to another house. However, if they have to have it, proceed. The first step was discussed above in the seller section: ask the listing agent what the seller is looking for in a buyer and what provisions are appealing to the seller. The same issues on price, terms, loan qualification, closing date and emotional tugs apply. Then, ask a broad question: "Is there anything else that is important to the seller?" Listen well, and take notes. The more of the desired terms that you give the seller, the more likely you will be the successful suitor, because some bidding wars are decided on how easy it is to work with the buyer, and the buyer's agent. You need to focus on much more than the price so try to give the seller everything that will make them happy.

What procedure?

The next thing you need to know is what procedure the seller's agent is going to follow to respond to all of the offers. If the agent says they are just going to negotiate with one buyer at a time, you need to find out what will make your client that buyer. Some agents negotiate with the first offer that comes in, so be the first in time. Others select one offer based on quality. Whatever the criteria, find out what it takes. Make a mental note that the listing agent probably has little experience in multiple offers, because this procedure is poor representation of the seller, but it is the easiest for the listing agent. If that is what the listing agent is going to do, you need to play their game.

If the seller is going to give counter offers to the best qualified buyers, provide the best qualifications you can. If the seller is going to negotiate with all the buyers at once, be sure you get to stay in the game to get a chance at the property.

How many offers?

The most important information is how many buyers are making offers. At one point in 2004, my California team lost six bidding wars where we represented buyers. So, we studied what it took to win these wars, and rarely lost again.

If you are going to be the successful bidder, you will need to go over the asking price unless there are very few offers by agents who are not accustomed to bidding wars. Call the listing agent a short time before they are going to consider the offers and find out how many offers there are. The price you need is proportional to the number of buyers. The more buyers there are, the higher the price. You want to come in right before the deadline so that you know about the other offers, but other agents do not know about yours.

If you are in an area where multiple offers are not common, you may have a hard time convincing your buyer to offer more than the asking price. Many buyers think that the asking price is more than the seller wants, and they just won't go that high. However, the abundance of buyers and multiple offers show that the home is easily worth the asking price and probably worth more. You will not get that level of interest in an overpriced home. Furthermore, having multiple bidders show it is either underpriced or the market is rising so rapidly that the contract you get at a high price today will be below market price when it closes in 30 to 60 days.

Even by going over the asking price, your buyer will have made a good investment so long as you do not get too carried away by the auction effect on the price. If the buyer is worried about overpaying, put in an appraisal contingency so that they can be protected by a disinterested appraiser's opinion of the value of the property. However, you will need to explain to the buyer that this contingency will make your offer less appealing, as it gives your buyer a chance to terminate the sale if the appraisal does not come in at the contract price.

When I represent sellers with multiple offers, I put the offers with appraisal contingencies in a lower category than offers without that contingency, as I want to select a buyer who is sure to close at the price offered. The power to terminate the sale if it does not appraise gives the buyer the power to try to renegotiate the price to the amount of the appraisal, so the seller can lose the premium price. In short, tell your buyer that the only way you will win the bidding with an appraisal contingency in your contract is if everyone else has an appraisal contingency in their contract or if the agent representing the seller does not understand the power of that contingency.

Ability to close the sale

It is crucial to show the seller that your client can close the sale—absolutely, for certain, no ifs, ands or buts. Follow the example above about furnishing bank statements. Be sure that key information is blanked out to protect your client from identity theft problems and be careful how you transmit this information, as email is not secure. You have to show more financial strength than the competition. It is wonderful if your buyer is paying all cash because the issues with the financing are eliminated. If your buyer needs a loan, provide as complete a loan approval as possible. Think of the process as a horse race. The sellers are trying to pick the right horse, one that is certain to cross the finish line. You want to convince the sellers that if they bet on you, they will not be sorry.

Use emotion

Representing a buyer in a bidding war is a great time to use emotion to your advantage with the seller.

> *In 2004, I was standing in the kitchen of a vacant house in Rancho Palos Verdes with my clients, writing a great offer. I knew that multiple offers had been submitted, so I called the listing agent to see what terms we could put in the offer to make it more appealing. He said the seller had made a decision to select another buyer and would not consider any other offers, even though she had not signed a contract. We told him our offer would be the top price, that the buyers definitely had the financing and would close quickly. He said the seller would not budge. I found out after the sale closed that the agent representing the successful buyers had submitted a picture of their daughters with their offer. The seller had grown up in that house, and one of the girls in the picture reminded the seller of herself as a little girl. The seller wanted that little girl to grow up in her house. The successful offer contained enough money, so the seller would not listen to more money once she had made up her mind on an emotional basis.*

Take It "As Is"

One other way to separate your buyer from the others is to commit to taking the home "as is" while retaining the right to inspect the house. If you feel that there is a good chance you will get the home, get a professional inspection before making an offer, and attach your inspection to your offer to take it "as is." Many agents have had buyers promise to take a home "as is" then lost the sale when the selected buyers experienced buyer's remorse about the high price they paid and tried to claim that the subsequent inspection showed problems they did not expect. At that point these buyers try to ask for repairs, and the agents get into a battle over the "as is" provisions of the contract. In other words, experienced agents do not believe that all buyers will honor the "as is" clause. However, if your buyer has the inspection done before the offer, the seller is more confident that you will not have a change of heart between signing the contract and the close of the sale because the buyer cannot claim any surprise from an inspection that occurs after the agreement on the price.

How to represent a buyer: A Case Study

Myron Spell with Prudential Carolinas Realty in Raleigh, North Carolina, won a bidding war on a home down the street from my house in Raleigh, North Carolina. The home was not in good condition and had been on the market for awhile. Myron knew there were several offers on the property, because the new agent who took over the listing dropped the price way below the market value to get it sold quickly. He convinced the listing agent to delay the response to any of the offers until he had an inspection done on the property. The inspection revealed a number of problems, all of which the buyers could live with. The first thing Myron did right was to find out that there were three other offers on the property and get his buyer to make an offer over the asking price. After the sale closed, he learned that the other offers were equal to or less than the asking price.

The next thing he did right was to prove that his buyers would take the property "as is" because they attached a copy of the inspection report to their offer. Attaching the inspection report provided a negotiating bonus to his clients, because the seller is now on notice of all of the defects in the property and the listing agent would need to disclose those defects to the other potential buyers. Since the report showed the house was not in wonderful condition, the disclosure decreased the other buyers' interest in the house. With the other offers being lower or equal in price—and none of them were "as is"—the seller did not even give any of the bidders a counter offer. They just accepted the offer presented by Myron's clients.

Win Before the Auction

A completely different buyer strategy is to try to change the listing agent's procedure for dealing with multiple offers so that you win before anyone else gets a chance at the property. Present your offer as early as possible, hopefully before anyone else has an offer on the table. If the agent says other agents have said they are going to write an offer, remind the agent how many times agents claim that they are going to present an offer but do not come through. In your offer, put a short time limit for the seller to consider it, well before other agents can submit their offers. Make an offer that is exceptional on the price and gives the seller the terms that they want. Then make your offer contingent on the seller not considering any other offers, i.e. if they give counter offers to anyone else, your offer is withdrawn. If you establish your buyer as extremely well qualified, ready to close "as is," and give the seller everything else they want, the seller may not be willing to take the chance of losing your offer on the hope that others will be presented.

Now that you know how to excel when there are multiple offers, you need to become an expert at negotiating repairs.

CHAPTER 12

NEGOTIATING REPAIRS

Real estate agents refer to negotiating repairs as the second round of negotiations. When you are negotiating the original agreement, the balance of power is usually somewhat equal between the buyer and seller, depending on the market and the motivation of the parties. However, after an agreement is reached the seller's mindset shifts from a position of questioning the original deal to supporting the completion of the agreement. As the seller releases his emotional attachment to the home and makes plans to move, the seller's commitment to the completion of the deal strengthens.

On the other side of the transaction, the buyer frequently gets a case of buyer's remorse, wondering if they did the right thing and whether the price is too high. So the buyer's commitment to the sale decreases and their ability to walk away increases. In most states, if the seller does all the repairs the contract goes forward, but if they refuse to do even one item, the buyer has a chance to cancel the agreement. If a sale falls through, the seller may have to disclose all the items that the inspection report called out as problems to any new buyers. When the home appears back on the market, it is frequently treated as damaged goods by the other real estate agents. These are some of the reasons that shift the dynamics of the negotiations so that the seller is at a disadvantage when negotiating repairs.

This second round of negotiations is the most frustrating for real estate agents, as they are not putting a deal together but rather trying to hold on to one. Plus, spending your time arguing over the quality of the splash blocks under the downspouts is not a high dollars-per-hour job. You do not want to gloss over any item that may be a repair issue, as full disclosure is necessary, but you do not want to make a mountain out of a mole hill. If you have a team with a closing coordinator to handle the sale from the signing of the contract to the closing of the transaction, you may want to teach them how to negotiate the repair issues

Negotiating Repairs For the Seller

If you represent the seller, there are several ways to be a good counselor. You can have the seller get a home inspection before the house is put on the market and either make the repairs or be ready to disclose the information in the inspection. I recommend making the repairs because:

- the home will show better with everything in good condition;
- the buyer will think any necessary repairs are more expensive than they really are because most real estate agents overestimate the cost of fixing something because they have been burned every time they have underestimated a cost;
- having a long list of items to disclose gives the buyer too much support for their negotiations to reduce the price during the initial negotiations, or after the disclosure is delivered, if you are in a state like California;
- having many disclosed defects gives the buyer a bad impression of the quality of the house.

If the seller is not willing to do all the repairs, I recommend that you do not have an inspection before listing the house. This means the seller has to take care of repairs on short notice in the short time between the inspection and the close of the sale, resulting in higher prices for the repairs. However, this disadvantage is outweighed by the marketing problems caused by disclosing defects in the house.

Whether you have had a pre-listing inspection or not, during the course of the negotiations, help the seller understand that there will be some costs to the repairs, and try to get a high enough sales price to allow the seller to do the repairs from the sale proceeds. When the repairs cost about what was expected, or less, the sale proceeds smoothly. Surprises that cost significantly above the amount expected means you need to let the seller adjust to the bad news, then proceed.

You can try to minimize the amount of repairs when you first reach agreement, particularly if the price is exceptionally low, by pointing out to the buyer that there will be no money available to make any marginal repairs. A good analogy is to say if they pay for a first-class airline ticket, they get to sit in the good seats and get special treatment. If they pay for coach, like they did with their low price, they do not get first-class treatment on repairs. You can even say that there are no funds for any repairs at all.

I have found that this rarely works, as most buyers and their agents forget that you did them a favor when the seller agreed to their low price. A buyer's agent asking for everything the inspector has on his list usually will say that their clients feel that the ridiculous items they are requesting are essential to their happiness. The coup de grace is when they say, "And I have to do what my buyer wants." It is true you have to follow your buyer's interest, but you should have some client control if you are a professional. One request sticks in my mind from the buyer who wanted us to clean the gutters—twice—after the agent promised that they would only ask for serious structural repairs.

If you do want to get a concession on repairs at the time the seller makes a concession on the price, you need to get an "as is" clause in the agreement. The buyer can still inspect the house and terminate the contract if the home does not meet expectations, so they are not buying "a pig in a poke," i.e. having to accept the house no matter what the condition. Most bank-owned property is sold this way.

> *I had an REO (for Real Estate Owned by the bank) listing in Clayton, North Carolina that had a defective well pump and problems with the heating and air conditioning, so the buyer wanted to ask the bank to make repairs in spite of the "as is" clause. I mentioned that this would reopen the negotiations on the price—and that we had a "back up" offer from another buyer who wanted the property badly. The buyer decided to skip the request for repairs and close on the sale as written.*

If you are representing a seller who has multiple offers, you may want to get a concession that the successful buyer will take the property "as is" for two reasons. First, you want protection against the buyer who outbid the field wanting to get something to compensate for having paid top dollar; they often ask for extensive upgrades and repairs before closing. Second, you want to protect your seller, who has other possible buyers and should have the option to select another one who will take it "as is," so long as the other buyer is competitive with the first choice.

The problem with the "as is" clause for most buyers is that their agents cannot handle the emotional reaction to the clause. Many buyers take the request to sell the property "as is" as an indication that there are serious problems with the house, and their imaginations run wild. I have found that it is normally better to deal with some ridiculous repair requests than to have the deal fall apart at the start because of a counter offer with an "as is" clause. Besides, you may have few repairs, and the agent for the buyer may be one who can control their clients.

Another way to deal with an unreasonable list of repair requests is to remember Nancy Reagan and "just say No." Some buyers will accept that, while others will come back with a shorter list, and still others will walk away.

Negotiating Repairs For the Buyer

Setting reasonable expectations is critically important when representing a buyer in the repair stage. There is no such thing as a perfect house. I have sold hundreds of houses, and I have had only one inspection that did not raise any issues. This includes new homes by some premier quality builders. The inspectors will find something, even if it is only to justify their fee.

The inspection industry standards for what an inspector must put in the report are different from the standards found in the purchase contract. The inspector must report everything he finds, even if it is only to warn about wear. The standards for repair issues in real estate contracts vary from state to state, as the terms of the contracts are different. Many real estate sales contracts require an item to be "in need of immediate repair" to warrant a request for repairs. In that case, the roof that is nearing the end of its useful life needs to be disclosed by the inspector, but the contract does not require repair by the seller so long as it is not leaking. Similarly, many of us have had the experience of having the buyer want a new water heater when the inspector says it is working fine, but it is old and nearing the end of its useful life. Explaining up front the difference between the standards of the inspection and the standards of the purchase contract helps the buyer read the inspection in a more discerning manner. The inspector is trying to tell them everything about the house, not just those items that qualify to be repaired under the contract.

One of the professional obligations of a buyer's agent is to discuss the request for repairs with the buyer. A good way to frame the subject is to explain that the inspection is to check that you are getting what you were expecting when you signed the contract, not to renegotiate the contract. Follow Rule 12 in Chapter 8: Don't Let Your Clients Do Something Really Stupid. If the buyer makes an insulting request for repairs, the seller will find some way to return the favor during the course of the contract and the closing. For example, when the buyer wants to move some items into the property before closing after making an insulting request for repairs, the seller will claim that the attorneys have advised against it and that a buyer occupancy agreement before closing is completely out of the question. If the buyer is not ready to close on time after being ridiculous about the repairs, the cost for the extension of the closing date will be exorbitant. Consider whether it is truly in your buyer's best interest to stretch the repairs to include a couple of maintenance items but to lose the ability to contact the seller after the sale to find out how to operate some of the electronics in the media room.

Try to minimize the appearance of your request for repairs if you represent the buyer. For example, write up your request about plumbing issues by specifying a particular page of the report instead of listing every faucet that drips. The short list of a few repairs seems more palatable than a document that goes on for pages listing every little item. When you present your request for repairs, emphasize the items that you did not ask for, so that you can get credit for the concessions that you have already made to the seller.

Negotiating with the Inspector

You never want an inspector to skip an item that he wants to put in a report. Do not try to negotiate with the inspector to leave anything out. It will come back to haunt you, as the failure to disclose is the largest source of litigation in real estate sales and a violation of the National Association of REALTORS® Code of Ethics. And when lawyers get involved, the cost of fixing a problem goes up, some say by a factor of ten.

You can, however, negotiate with the impression that the inspector is giving the buyer, particularly if you represent the seller and are dealing with an inspector who is trying to show how smart he is by making a big deal out of everything. Play to the inspector's implicit need to be the smartest person in the room by asking "How would you advise them to correct that?" When the explanation of the correction shows how easy it is to deal with the problem, you will have lessened the buyer's concern about the condition of the house.

However, there may be times when that won't work. In those cases, you will do well to find a tactful way to deal with any issues immediately as they arise.

For example, I have dealt with an inspector in Raleigh who would write up long lists of unnecessary items and who had the talent to make the problems seem much larger than they were. I started taking my tools to the inspection. As he found windows that did not open smoothly and started to launch into how dangerous that could be in a fire, I would take out my putty knife to unstick the window then spray silicone on it to make it work smoothly--one less item for the report. By the end of his inspection, I had time to fix dozens of little items and I had him check to see that they were properly repaired. So, instead of 48 items that would scare the buyer and infuriate the seller, there was only the normal 10 to 15. Also, the buyer liked the fact that they were getting immediate attention to improvements on their future house.

The better way to deal with potential issues with the inspector is to educate your seller on the items that are usually a focus of the inspection, so that they can repair them before the inspection if they need work. In other words, give your client the putty knife and silicone and let them get their windows unstuck.

My favorite education on this point was one tiny piece of wood with termintes on the ground under a wood deck. The home was free of termites and the piece of wood was eight feet from the house and six feet below the deck. But the seller had to do a termite treatment to satisfy the legislation on termite control, as the buyer's lender required complete compliance, even though the buyer thought this was ridiculous.

The talent for negotiating well is extremely important when you are negotiating repairs. If you are talented, the issues are solved easily and you close the sale gracefully. If not, the sale blows up over what should have been a little repair work.

Now that you can keep the sale together, you need to improve your talent at negotiating commissions so you can get well paid for your work.

CHAPTER 13

NEGOTIATING FOR YOUR OWN INCOME

This chapter covers the income you make from listing agreements, referral agreements, and buyer's agency agreements. These are situations in which real estate agents may negotiate commissions. The ability to negotiate commissions well has the most dramatic effect on how much profit you can make in your business, as you can make more money on the same sale. Similarly, negotiating buyer's agency agreements with your buyers provides loyalty and more of a guarantee that you get paid when they buy a property.

As far as your own income is concerned, you do not get what you deserve; you get what you negotiate.

Negotiating Listing Commissions

Real estate commissions are highly negotiable. Real estate as a profession is one of the most creative in offering different models of service that provide for different amounts of payment. There are firms that charge a flat fee for limited service, such as just putting your home in the Multiple Listing Service. There are discount firms that charge a lesser percentage commission in return for less service. There are real estate agents who provide a menu of service, and you select the items you want and get charged appropriately. There are full-service real estate agents who negotiate their commission down from what they would like to charge. There are also full-service real estate agents who charge more than their peers and insist on a premium over the amount other agents charge. Just a cursory look in any city will reveal a large range of business models to show that real estate agents negotiate their commissions in many ways.

Concentrate on value

One of the best ways to negotiate the commission on a listing is to provide such an image of marketing, service, and advice that the clients would not ask you to negotiate your commission. In other words, if the perceived value of what is offered is high, the client will not want to negotiate the price, as it could go up. When someone wants to trade you their $50 bill for your $20 bill, you do not open up negotiations to try to get a better deal. So explain the features of your marketing, the exceptional services you provide, and the benefit of your negotiating skills to give the client an appreciation of the value.

There are a number of agents who have such a strong reputation and high demand for their services that they can command a premium over other agents. One way they accomplish this is through the basic principle of supply and demand. These agents restrict the supply of their service by only taking a certain number of listings, because if you are a solo agent there are only so many listings you can service and creating a team to handle more listings could be more expensive than it is worth. As long as there is more demand for their services than the limited supply, the price of their service remains at a premium. Margaret Rome, a real estate agent in Baltimore, Maryland, has been able to get a premium on her commissions, as she has been able to keep the image of her services high while she is careful about the number of listings she will take. As long as the demand is high, the commission can also be high if you negotiate well.

One of the major aspects in establishing your value is instilling the fear of loss in a client. Choosing the wrong real estate agent puts a large strain on a family when the move is uncertain and filled with problems. Having the wrong agent can also cause a financial disaster. Most sellers are afraid of making the wrong choice. You need to use that fear as part of presenting the value of your service, because part of what you are selling is security, protection, and freedom from fear.

Confidence

Brodow's Law from *Negotiation Bootcamp* is to be willing to walk away, always. The seller will sense if you are desperate. They will also sense if you are willing to walk away. Convey your interest in listing their property, but also show your willingness to walk away in order to strengthen your bargaining position. Some real estate agents believe that if they do not negotiate their commissions, they will lose their customers. The more successful agents believe the opposite: That if they do not defend their commission, the seller will lose respect for them. The seller's perception is that if you will cut your commission to below the market value, you may be worth less than market value.

Many sellers just have to ask if you will negotiate your commission. If you say no, they will go on to another subject. Since most of the communication in the spoken word is the tone you use and the way you hold your body, use tone and body language to your advantage. Don't just say "No," but say it with a hint that you are surprised that they asked and a touch of a chuckle implying "How could you?" It is a form of a flinch.

My favorite statement to bring the point home is "You do not want me to cut my commission." Then wait for them to ask why. The answer is, "If your agent is such a weak negotiator that they give their own money away, how well will they do when an offer comes in and they are negotiating with your money?" If you want to show some style, change the subject to ask what circumstances would make the seller feel that she should pay you a bonus. When the seller gets you to give up the bonus, they see some value in the concession and may give up their discussion of cutting the commission.

When the seller says, "But Bob from Bob's Realty will do it for much less," they are using a technique called a squeeze. The appropriate response is to say that you are sorry that Bob has so little faith in his service that he realizes it is not worthy of a realistic payment. You need to point out that the difference in the quality of service far exceeds the difference in the price. Never apologize for your position that you are entitled to earn a reasonable living; just present your position with confidence.

Another approach is to use the higher authority technique. Indicate that your firm has a policy of charging a particular commission, so you cannot lower the commission for them, as you would have to lower the commission for everyone. A good phrase to add is that if you could cut your commission, the people you would do it for is them. But you cannot. Some sellers may accept that you do not have the authority to reduce the commission.

Explain in Detail

Some sellers need more than a simple no, as they feel that "no" is just your starting position. If they want to really get into the discussion, explain how the commission is divided. Since real estate agents cannot even give the appearance of trying to have a uniform commission rate, let's use an unusual number in the example. The classic is to take out however many dollar bills there are for your commission, e.g., if it is an 8 percent commission, take out eight one-dollar bills. Then, take half of them away, explaining that they go to the agent who sells the property. Take away some for your split with your firm, or the "desk rent" that you pay. Take some more away for your marketing costs. Take some more away for office, transportation and other expenses. Then explain that what they are really asking is to take an amount that is more than what is available for you to support your family. This gives you no reason to do a good job for them.

You also need to make the seller aware that a portion of the commission goes to the agent for the buyer. If the listing agent cuts the commission, and cuts the amount that is paid to the agent for the buyer, how excited will agents for the buyers be to show the property? A property that is offered at a reduced commission gets less attention, particularly in a buyer's market.

Set Aside

Another way to deal with commission negotiations is to set the issue aside. Explain that you and the seller are a team, both in this effort together. You depend on them to have a good house in good condition that is available for showings at reasonable times. They depend on you to get the attention of potential buyers, make them appreciate the special features of the home, and negotiate the offers. If you end up with a great price, you are in it together, as there is enough money to go around. If you end up with a price that is unreasonably low, then you will both be disappointed together, as they will take less money—and so will you.

Explain that now is not the time to negotiate the commission as you have not been given a chance to bring in a good offer and prove your worth. If you do, you earn the full commission. If you don't, you work with them at that time on the amount of the commission. Setting aside the issue until later has worked for me, as I have yet to have anyone want to negotiate the commission after seeing how much work our Team has done to sell the house. If you happen to do a less-than-wonderful job and want to share in the loss with your client, there are worse ways to resolve a client's disappointment than by reducing some of your commission.

Before you reduce your commission, though, ask more questions to see if that is the real issue. If the seller is looking for a certain amount of net proceeds, you may be able to set the issue aside, as you may get those proceeds if the property sells well. If you uncover the seller's needs, you may find another way to satisfy that need instead of reducing your income. It may be that the seller just needs to vent frustration over the cost of the process, so you may have to give the seller enough acceptance time to adjust their expectations.

The opposite of the set aside is when the seller wants to think it over before listing the property. The more the delay, the more likely the commission negotiating is going to come up again. So when the seller wants to sleep on it, start asking questions and apologize for not making everything clear. "I am sorry I did not answer all your questions. What issues do you need to think about?" Some people will not decide while you are there, but it is worth the effort to bring the negotiations to a conclusion and sign the papers before you leave. A fall-back position is to say you will fill out the paperwork and leave it with them with their signatures on it. If they decide to go forward, you will pick them up. If they decide not to, they can rip them up. When they have committed the effort to filling out the papers, many times they will decide to have you take the paperwork with you so you can proceed with the listing.

If You Have To Negotiate the Commission

If you want to approach the negotiations differently, you can create several levels of service and offer a menu of services that the seller may choose. If the seller wants to pay a lower amount, have that be at one of the lower levels of service.

Sellers may start at the lowest level of service. Then they may call up asking you to do something more to market the home, if the home does not sell immediately. If that item is on the higher level of service, ask if they want to upgrade to that level of service, which also goes with an increased commission. You did not "upsell" them to get a higher commission; they wanted that extra service.

If you do not use the set aside, have a frank discussion that this time is the only time you and your clients will be negotiating the commission. Once the commission is set, you are going ahead with an abundance of work based on the commitment they are making to you. Just as you will not fail to do what you promise, you do not want them to renege on their promise. This will help keep clients from asking you to throw in the money to close the gap between what they want out of a sale and what the buyer offers—though you will get some clients who will try this anyway.

If you are going to cut your commission, try to negotiate it in dollars, not percent. After all, a 1 percent reduction on a 6 percent commission is actually a 17 percent reduction in the commission. Have the sellers ever gotten a 17 percent reduction when they negotiate to buy a car? The commission rate will vary, as there is no standard commission rate, so use whatever is appropriate for you. Many sellers are looking for a 1 percent reduction in the commission, as 1 percent does not sound like a lot to them. But to you, it may be 1 percent of $1,600,000 which is $16,000. If you talk with them in dollars, they may be happy with a $5,000 reduction in the commission, as it sounds like a serious amount of money.

Another way to negotiate the commission is to throw in an additional benefit to justify leaving the commission alone. Offer to hire an ASHI-approved home inspector for a pre-listing inspection or to provide a home warranty to the buyer as a part of your package. If the seller gets that small concession, that victory may be enough to end the discussion of commissions.

Negotiating Listings When a Discount Broker is an Option

Some of the sellers you are meeting are considering discount real estate brokers, which may be right for some sellers. If you are a full-service real estate agent, you will need to negotiate with sellers who are considering these types of services.

One of the biggest items to discuss is to be sure the seller is aware of the difference in the service. If you are a master at negotiations, walk the seller through the difference in the amount of money they will receive if you negotiate a good price versus the discount brokerage, many of which do not handle negotiations at all. So, if the seller is prepared to face the buyer's professional negotiator without any professional assistance, or with limited help from a discount agent, they may want to consider discount service. Some statistical research of your list-to-sell ratio (the difference between your listing prices and selling prices) and the list-to-sell ratio of the discount firm would show how much money the seller would lose by employing a discount firm. One of the reasons for the poor list-to-sell ratio for discount firms is that many real estate agents reduce their offers to sellers represented by discount firms—first, because they know the seller has saved money on the commission, and second, because they may be facing an inexperienced agent or an agent who cannot spend much time on negotiations, as discount firms function well only if their volume is high.

The other differences in service depend on what you do for your listings. If you have a dramatic Internet presence—which is where over 80 percent of the buyers start looking for a home—the seller will get more exposure, which will result in a higher price. All the other marketing efforts should be discussed. The other services, such as staging consultations, access to repair contractors, concierge service, inspection assistance, and closing coordination, also need to be detailed so that the seller gets a fair comparison. Your knowledge of the contracts, the proper procedures for handling repair requests, and your ability to negotiate your way from the initial offer to the final settlement should be mentioned, as well as your service after the sale.

It is important to make the price comparison as accurate as possible. Some discount brokerages concentrate on the small fee they charge to put the property in the MLS and other limited services. You need to point out that the seller will also be paying the agent who brings the buyer a commission. So, instead of looking at a 1.5 percent commission to the listing agent only, the seller is actually looking at a 3.9 percent commission for the sum of the commissions to the listing agent and the agent for the buyer. Be sure the comparison between your commission and the discount commission is comparing apples to apples, including the fee to the buyer's agent. When you do that, the discount firm shows less of a savings when you consider all the costs. Be sure to point out that if the seller offers less of a commission to the agent for the buyers than the amount offered by other homes on the market, it may affect the number of agents who are willing to show the home.

Point out that a traditional broker only gets paid when the property sells, while the discount broker frequently gets up-front fees. As a result, traditional brokers have a vested interest in getting the property sold, and the difference in this motivation may mean the difference between selling and not selling.

My negotiating strategy concerning discount competition was quoted in Bernice Ross's *Waging War on Real Estate's Discounters*. I sell expired listings after other agents have failed to get them sold. I noticed that the listings of discount brokerages expired more often than other listings did. So when I meet with a seller who was considering a discount broker, I bring the statistics on that firm. When I show him that virtually none of my listings expire and several of theirs have failed to sell, I ask the seller how much he would save by having his home remain on the market for an extended period of time, then come back on the market as "damaged goods" when it did not sell. The long days on market period has to be shown in most Multiple Listing Services, and buyers lower their offers for homes that have been on the market for a long time. The amount of the additional cost in having an expired listing overwhelms the savings from going with the discount broker.

The best way for me to illustrate the difference is the experience of my clients, Rod and Cassandra. I sold their home in North Raleigh. Rod's company folded, so they had a financial problem. They had purchased the house a short time before, and it would not sell for enough to pay off the entire loan and a full commission. They also purchased it from a business partner and without representation by a real estate agent, and they paid a price that was high for the neighborhood. They decided to try a discount broker, which made sense mathematically, as the sale price could be enough to cover the discount commission and the loan. They were trying to do the right thing with the information they had. But when the house did not sell, they contacted me.

At first, I tried to sell the house for enough to cover the loan and commissions. In spite of my best efforts, there were few showings. So we had to reduce the price. Cassandra said they did not have the money to pay off the rest of the loan to the bank, so I explained "short sales," which I have been doing since the 1990s. She had heard that she would have to pay income tax on the amount that they did not pay back to the bank. Federal legislation in 2007 allows a homeowner to pay less than what is owed on their mortgage and not pay income tax on the "short" amount due the bank, under certain situations. They appeared to qualify under that legislation.

With the discount broker and a price no one would pay, Cassandra and Rod would get nothing out of not selling and would have no income tax consequences (although there might be some tax problems coming out of a foreclosure). With my reduced price that buyers loved, Cassandra and Rod would get nothing out of the sale, have no income tax consequences, and the house would be sold so the problem would be gone. We reduced the price enough to get three offers, which bid the price back up. Then I had to navigate through months of short sale review with the bank. The bank wanted to turn the short sale down because they got an appraisal that said the house was worth $100,000 more than the sales price. (You would think that a bank would question that appraisal, as the house had been on the market for about a year, priced well under what the appraisal said it was worth.)

I would not let the bank turn it down without using every tool I had. I contacted the guarantor of the loan, i.e. the company that would actually take the loss on the short sale. I negotiated with the loss mitigation expert there, convincing her that the appraisal was wrong by sending her a huge volume of market analysis. When the guarantor said they would approve the sale, the bank had to go along with it. The best part of the sale occurred when Cassandra called me screaming for joy, then crying, when I got the sale approved and solved her problem. She even sent me a text message from the hospital after her child was born thanking me again.

The detail in this example is to show that a discount broker might not have been able to do this, as it took my 29 years of experience, months of my time, and every ounce of my negotiating ability to accomplish the result. The result did not cost Cassandra and Rod anything, but the difference was it got the home sold and off their back. In certain circumstances, if sellers try to pay too little for real estate services, they are making a choice that will result in the job not getting done.

Negotiating Referral Fees

If you refer a client to another real estate agent, be sure to call first to discuss the referral fee. Obviously, negotiate the referral fee before you give the other agent the referral. Follow the rule about letting the other person make the first offer by asking what they send as referral fees. If it is higher than you would have asked, enjoy it. If it is lower, I explain the amount that I send to the other agent when I receive a referral and add that I usually receive the same amount that I send. Every now and then there is a reason for the fee to be lower than my usual one, so I listen to the other agent's reasons. But before you just accept their lower number, try a little nibble to increase it some.

Relocation companies provide buyers and sellers to agents and take a referral fee. It is difficult to negotiate the amount of the referral fee with these firms, as they are bureaucratic. Typically they have a certain fee that they require, and if you will not accept it, they will find someone else who will. One of the best ways to negotiate is for your client to insist to their relocation counselor they use your services. To keep the "transferee" interested in the job transfer, the relocation firm is more motivated to work with you. Show the additional services you provide and their additional costs to you for those services. Then, suggest a more appropriate referral fee. Get ready for a bureaucratic response, with a reference to a higher authority who is not cooperating. If you get that response, negotiate directly with the higher authority.

When referral fees were 20 percent to relocation companies, many agents were willing to pay the referral fee to the relocation company in return for the additional business. When they went up to 25 percent, they were still acceptable, as many agents send other agents 25 percent referral fees. The increase to 30 percent, however, caused many of the more successful agents to refuse to take relocation listings, and the increase to 35 percent sped up that trend. After all, if you have a cost to run your business that is about 50 percent of your gross commission income, and you give away 35 percent of the gross commission, it does not leave much left over. If the transferee will lead to additional business as a great source of referrals, it may be worth it. Otherwise, you may want to concentrate on other parts of your business.

Negotiating Buyer's Agency Agreements

In general, the real estate agent works for the seller. Since purchasing a house requires negotiation, the buyer needs to hire the real estate agent as a buyer's agent. The rules of the buyer's agency agreement change from state to state, so we can only discuss general rules here. It is up to you to learn what your local laws and regulations are regarding buyer's agency, as well as to obtain the local buyer's agency agreement, normally available through the association of real estate agents for your state.

Why buyers should sign a buyer's agency agreement

The simplest way to explain the benefits of a buyer's agency agreement is in terms of representation, loyalty, and counseling. Any buyer who wants the agent to be loyal to the buyer needs an agreement to shift the normal rules of agency so that the agent works for the buyer, which means that the agent's loyalty is to the buyer and that the agent provides counseling that is in the buyer's best interest.

An easy way to show the benefit of this shift in loyalty to a buyer is to explain what happens if the seller or the seller's agent asks questions of the agent. If there is no buyer's agency agreement, the agent needs to tell the seller everything they know about the buyer, including how much they are willing to pay for the house. So, a buyer who wants to keep information confidential needs to sign a buyer's agency agreement so the agent will tell the seller that everything known about the buyer is confidential.

Since the agent gets paid only if the buyer is loyal and buys something through that agent, the agent is going to work the hardest and bring the best deals to the people who have signed buyer's agency agreements.

Plain and simple, the people who do not want to commit to an agent will see the same lack of commitment and loyalty from the agent. I use the analogy of going steady: The agent is committed to giving them the best service, and the buyers are committed to the agent. The buyer gets an agent who will work hard for the buyer, and the agent is assured of getting paid.

How long a commitment?

Some agents want to tie up the buyer forever, which is a hard bargain to negotiate. I prefer "easy exit" agreements, where the buyer can terminate the relationship at any time before an offer is presented or accepted. That way, the buyer does not feel trapped, and the agent has to prove their worth every day. Again, I use the going steady analogy. You can break up at any time, for any reason, or for no reason. Even better than going steady, when you break up, you do not have to give the ring back, since the buyer keeps the benefit of the service until then.

Who pays the buyer's agent?

The standard buyer's agency agreements specify that the buyer takes on the obligation to pay the agent a specified amount or percentage of the purchase price, and the agent will first look to the seller to get that amount satisfied. If the seller pays enough, the buyer does not have to pay anything. If the seller does not pay enough, the buyer has to pay the rest. Many buyers are reluctant to pay their agent, as the tradition has been that the agents are fully paid by the seller.

I used to be a wimp when it came to asking a buyer to pay me. In order to get the commitment of a buyer's agency agreement, I would specify that "All commissions are paid by the seller, the buyer pays nothing for agent's representation at the close of the sale." Using the going steady analogy, I was so desperate for the relationship that I would let my counterpart walk all over me. I would even fill in the blank on the form with a zero where it said how much the buyer was to pay if they purchased from a For Sale By Owner or other seller who did not offer a commission. After one buyer from New York rode one of my buyer's agents all over the county, signed a contract with a builder that took days to negotiate, then found another property that they purchased without my agent's knowledge and cancelled the sale we had worked so hard on, we changed our practice. Now, our standard policy is to fill in the normal commission in the blank where it obligates the buyer to pay us if there is no commission offered by the seller. If the buyer does not want to do that, we may not want to provide our service, as this is how we support our families. The quality of our relationships has improved since we are only going steady with people who respect and understand our standards.

What about a deposit?

I like the idea of having the buyer give the agent a deposit that will be credited to the buyer when the sale closes. It is a tangible indication of commitment, as well as a practical way to keep the buyer loyal, because they will not get their deposit back if they do not buy a home with that agent. I have never been able to implement this idea because it is not customary in any of the markets where I work. In other words, the buyers think it is a strange request, since none of the other agents make that request. Because it makes the buyer feel that I am more interested in my financial gain than in their best interest, I have not pushed the concept. It is extremely important that my clients feel they can trust me, and that I will put their interests ahead of my own. Since the deposit does not go in that direction, I do not use it. However, it is becoming more common in some parts of the country, so you may want to consider this practice.

How much compensation?

As much as possible. I use the prevailing commission splits so that my prices are competitive with what the buyer can find elsewhere. If you can show that you provide extra service or extra value, ask for whatever the market will bear.

Some agents in my markets will give any bonuses or higher-than-normal commission payments paid by the seller to their buyer clients. I like that gesture, but I think it is something my buyer's agents have earned through years of hard work. Since I have never had a buyer ask for the bonus, I do not think it undermines the relationship to allow my buyer's agents to keep what they have earned. Other agents think it shows more commitment to the buyer to give them the bonus, so you may want to consider that approach. New laws in several states require you to disclose the bonus on the commission to the buyer before a contract is signed, so check your local regulations to be sure you are in compliance.

If you negotiate well for your own compensation, you will get paid well for your services. If you do not, you will have the same sale but less money for your listings and referrals. If you do not negotiate buyer's agency well, you may do an abundance of work and get no compensation at all.

One of the most important negotiating talents is to be able to negotiate a good living for yourself.

Now that you can negotiate with your clients, you need to improve your ability to have a profitable relationship with a real estate firm.

CHAPTER 14

NEGOTIATIONS BETWEEN REAL ESTATE FIRMS AND AGENTS

Some of the most important negotiations in real estate are between the real estate firm and an agent. The negotiations determine where the agent works, who the agent associates with on a daily basis, what "flag" the agent flies in presentations to the public, and how much money the firm and the agent make.

When deciding which firm to align yourself with, there are two critical aspects to take into consideration for the negotiations. First, know everything you can about the negotiator; in other words, preparation is critical. Second, know your limits, most importantly your other choices and your walk-away price. These lessons apply to the negotiator for the firm as well as the agent. We will discuss it from the point of view of the agent first, then from the point of view of the firm.

From the Viewpoint of the Agent

There are a number of options available to you when deciding which real estate firm to be affiliated with. One choice is not to affiliate at all—to be a sole practitioner, i.e. have your own one-person firm. The negotiations are easy: how much pain can you tolerate in return for keeping all of the gross commission income. (This choice is becoming more common in some areas of the country like North Carolina, where all real estate agents have to be licensed as brokers, i.e. they do not need to be supervised by a broker and so it is easier to have your own firm.) However, you get to do all the administrative work, particularly accounting for earnest money deposits and maintaining trust accounts, along with purchasing and maintaining all the equipment. This choice is an excellent one for a low-producing real estate agent, as a major firm will not offer you much money in return for associating with them. However, if you are a serious producer it can be in your interest to align yourself with a good firm so that they take care of all the administrative issues for much less than it will cost you to do those tasks yourself. Particularly when you start your career, you may need the image of the firm to take advantage of their marketing and reputation.

Compensation structure

One of the first things to consider when selecting a firm is the compensation structure. As always, the negotiations are won or lost by the research you do before you meet with the firm. There is every form of compensation imaginable between a firm and a real estate agent, from firms that split the commission with you, to firms that have "caps" on the maximum amount they will take, to firms that give you the vast majority of the commission but charge fees that are commonly referred to as "desk rent" to firms that claim to give you 100% of the commission in return for a fee.

You have to decide which compensation structure works best for you. If you are not sure you will make many sales, the firms that have no desk rent may be preferable even though they take more of each commission check. If you make a decent number of sales, paying desk rent and keeping more of each commission check may be better for you. This is one of the reasons many real estate agents start out with one firm, then change to another when their production changes.

Company volume, facilities and culture

Another part of reviewing the choices of firms is to see which ones produce most of the sales, and what type of sales they generate. I like to be associated with firms that create a lot of business, as I can pick up ideas from the other agents as well as pick up business that comes to an important firm. If you like to work with builders and selling new construction, go with the firms that have that type of business. If you generate your own business, associate with the firms that will give you the most support for your sales. If you want to work with corporate relocation, look for firms with productive relocation departments.

Before you meet with the broker, talk to some of the agents in the firm to see what the culture is like to determine if that is the kind of atmosphere you enjoy. The company's philosophy of doing business is important to review, as you will need a company whose policies are consistent with yours. You will have a steady stream of conflicts if you select a company where their procedures and ethics do not match yours. Also, the atmosphere of the office has a major effect on your work day.

Next, you need to figure out what you need from the firm. Do you need a large office with room for your team? Or, do you need no office space whatsoever, other than an occasional use of the meeting rooms? I have had the two extremes with my two Teams. In Raleigh, I have a large suite with RE/MAX United, as I need room for my administrative staff, office equipment, and a place for my buyer's agents. In Palos Verdes, with RE/MAX Palos Verdes, I had no space at their office at all, just the use of their conference rooms and a place to pick up my mail and receive offers. I had all the equipment I needed in my home office. In Raleigh, my staff prefers to work in an office setting. In Palos Verdes, the group was happier working from home offices. In short, you need to know your needs and wants before you sit down with the broker representing the firm. My advice is to keep your ego in check and don't pay too much for flashy offices, unless you feel the flashy office image will help with your clients.

Know the firm's negotiator

Once you have figured out what the choices are for the firms, get as much information as you can about the counterpart you will be dealing with. The Internet is a great resource. Google the broker to find out how they present themselves online. Look up their home in the tax records. Talk to people who know them, particularly people who have worked with them. Find out if they are visual or verbal, and what personality type they are. If you are presenting yourself to a visual person who is Marston's director (D) personality, you will use lots of graphics and get quickly to the point in your presentation. If you are talking to a verbal person with a Marston's compliant (C) personality, you will use lots of discussion with lots of details.

The vast majority of managers of real estate offices have the director (D) personality, the type of person who likes information in bullet points and wants to reach an agreement quickly. When in doubt, prepare for that style of presentation.

Practice negotiating

The best thing about negotiating with real estate firms is that there are so many of them. Practice on the ones that you do not think you want to be associated with, just to get your timing down and to improve your ability to negotiate face-to-face. Take notes of the important points during your meetings. You will be surprised at how reinforcing taking notes is, because the broker will think that whatever you write down is important to you. As a result, they will start to emphasize whatever causes you to write a note. After the practice meetings, look over your notes to be sure you can reconstruct the benefits and liabilities of working with that firm.

When you think you are ready, move on to the A list firms. You already know about dressing for success and having only one chance to make a good first impression. Adapt to your counterpart's communication style, so that they are more comfortable sharing information. Use what you have learned about collaborative negotiating to find out what is important to the firm and share what is important to you. Then, see if you can find the ingredients to a successful relationship where you can provide the firm the items that are critical to them while you get what you want.

How to choose

After the meeting, put the proposal you received in a spreadsheet and annotate it with the personal impressions of the advantages and disadvantages of the firm. Fill out the spreadsheet with the size of your office, the administrative charges and the percentage of the commission that will be yours, as well as any other deal points. Not everything about your choices will fit easily into the cells of a spreadsheet, as you will need to consider the culture, support, and intangibles. After you have had meetings with all the firms that fit your needs, you can compare them analytically in the spreadsheet and personally by looking at your notes. Then evaluate your information in line with what you know about yourself. Are there things that do not fit in this analysis on paper that are more important to you? For example, I stayed with one firm for much longer than I should have in terms of the money because the manager was extremely supportive, and the office staff made the work environment delightful.

When you have narrowed your choices down to a couple of firms, think about sharing your spreadsheet with your favorite firm. If one firm is better on paper, but you like the other one better, show the other one your alternatives, so that they will know what your other choices are. If they want you, they may stretch in order to get you to work with them.

Your value to the firm

Be sure to present the intangibles that you have to offer as a part of your benefit to the firm. If you can bring a talent to the office that will inspire the other agents, or solve problems that would arise in the office, they might want you more. For example, if you can negotiate Short Sales or have expertise in relocation, the firm may value those resources. If you can bring other agents to join the office, they will see value in that. If you can give a professional image to their firm, so that the other firms will see the firm as a more prestigious place, use that in your favor. If you are a well-established agent who creates a lot of sales, you can bring credibility to a firm. It is not just about money. It is about status and image.

> *A good example of this is when Allen Tate Realtors recruited Chris Yetter when it established its presence in Raleigh. Allen Tate has been a substantial presence in western North Carolina and was just moving into the Raleigh market. Mr. Yetter is a well respected agent who had been the President of the Raleigh Regional Association of REALTORS®. So, by having Chris Yetter join the firm, Allen Tate Realtors established more credibility.*

Once you have made your best deal with the best firm, be sure to properly document it. Most firms have large standard contracts that they want you to sign without modification. Do not fall prey to the feeling of legitimacy that comes from their standard form, as it was not written by "God's typewriter in the sky." Be sure to add an addendum to the contract to reflect the complete results of your negotiations and modify any provisions of the standard contract that are unacceptable. If the firm does not want to put all of the terms in writing, you should think twice about joining that firm, as you need a written record of what you are entitled to.

From the Viewpoint of the Real Estate Firm

The biggest factor in negotiating to have an agent join your firm is how badly your firm wants the agent. Most firms have a significant turnover, as the majority of new agents fail within the first three to five years. So firms are constantly recruiting, and some of them will accept anybody. On the one hand, you can look at agents as a commodity, since there is a ready supply of agents that you can recruit for your firm. A better approach is to focus on the good ones, as they will stay and prosper with your firm. Since nearly 80 percent of real estate agents leave the business in their first five years, finding the one in five that will succeed is valuable, because you will not have spent all the effort on training only to have them leave. When you consider that in most markets 10 percent of the agents do about 90 percent of the business, finding and retaining a top agent is critically important to the firm.

Preparation

The same two factors are important from the firm's point of view as from the agent's: (1) know who you are negotiating with, and (2) know your other choices and your walk-away price. If the agent is not new to the business. look on the Internet, because if they do not have an Internet presence, they lack one of the basic skills. On the Internet, see how they present themselves, what issues they focus on, and how their information is laid out. Look at their print advertising, and visit some of their listings to see how their brochures are done. Ask people who have worked with them about their personality, ethics, work habits and values. Basically, you are trying to find out what is important to them. If quality of work environment as well as high ethical standards and image for their office are important, prepare that information for your presentation. If it is all about money, get ready for that. If they are a newer agent, they are probably interested in training, lead generation, and other support that will further their development.

It's a business decision

A real estate firm is a business. You cannot give so much to one agent that you make no profit. If you do that on a regular basis, you will take everyone who relies on you out of the business. Figuring out when you will walk away from the financial demands of a potential recruit is critical. This is when you focus on selling the tangible benefits of working with your firm. For example, do you have an Internet lead-generating system that gives the agent leads either for free or for a referral fee? Do you have advertising campaigns that are no or low cost to the agent? You should also focus on "selling the invisible," i.e. the intangible benefits of being with your firm. Do you have a major brand that inspires consumer confidence? If so, the agent can benefit when they are competing for listings. Follow the rule of having more than one issue to negotiate; most agents make decisions on more issues than just money, so find a way to let the counterpart feel that they have won.

Some firms have a policy that they do not cut individual deals with each agent. They have a style of doing business, and will accept only agents who like that style, i.e. one size fits all. Others will adapt the proposal to tailor it to the needs of the individual agent. While this second style makes it more likely to get a deal with the agent, it also makes it more likely that you will be renegotiating with your existing agents as their needs change.

The two most important factors in negotiating with an agent are the level of expectations you create in the agent and respect for the issues raised by the agent. If you get the agent to expect more than what you are prepared to deliver, you will not succeed. So "underpromise" and "overdeliver," just like the agents do with their customers. Also, you have to respect the agent's time and pay attention to the agent's issues by being fully prepared and having productive meetings. Fitting your proposal to the agent is easier than reshaping the agent to meet your standard provisions.

The successful finish of negotiating a relationship with an agent is signing an agreement that completely documents the relationship. Just like in the section for agents, you need an addendum that modifies the standard contract to include all the terms that are important to your firm and the agent.

In all these chapters you have studied the art of real estate negotiating. Now, it is time to implement and practice.

CHAPTER 15

EPILOGUE

I hope you enjoyed this book. Now that you know what makes a good negotiator, you can become one. You understand all the terms and concepts that are used to develop the ability to negotiate better. By appreciating the different structures of negotiating, you can change the process to help your cause. You know how to prepare a game plan before you start, so you give your clients every opportunity to get to the results they desire. The principles and rules will guide you while the tools and techniques will give you what you need to succeed. Since you have made a detailed study of negotiating commissions, repairs, buyer's agency agreements and multiple offer strategies, you know what to do in detail in those situations. You even know how to negotiate with your firm.

This is highly valuable information. For example, using collaborative Win-win style of negotiating will make a major difference in your relationships, not only in business but with your family and friends. Practicing the principles and rules, and then applying the tools and techniques will make a major difference in your career.

Now it is time to move on to the next stage of developing your negotiating skills. In the same manner that you cannot become a ballerina just by reading a book, you cannot learn the touch, feel and finesse of negotiating just by reading this book. The book is a great start, as it puts you in touch with the ideas you need. Then, you have to practice these skills, review your successes, criticize your failures and develop your talent.

To practice and implement what you have learned, join the **Real Estate Negotiating Institute** found at **www.CreateAGreatDeal.com.** The members of the Institute provide an abundance of ideas, experiences, and solutions in real estate negotiating situations, as well as ongoing practice and training. There you can learn from everyone else's experience while you sharpen your tools and techniques as you take part in the discussion of real-life negotiating situations. By participating in the **Real Estate Negotiating Institute** you can open up the issues you are facing to the wisdom of the whole group, so you can have the best minds in the business help you solve recurring problems. Also, the support for your development from a friendly community makes improving your skills more fun.

I hope this book begins the process of creating a major improvement in your business. More importantly, I hope it improves the relationships among real estate agents and raises the level of talent in the real estate profession. If it does, the customers will have better experiences and real estate agents will get more respect, as well as more business.

Thank you for your interest in the art of real estate negotiating.

Definitions of "Negotiating"

"Negotiation is to seek mutual agreement through dialogue." Harvard Business Essentials, *Negotiation*, (Boston: HBS Press, 2003).

"Whenever people exchange ideas with the intention of changing relationships, whenever they confer for agreement, then they are negotiating." Gerard I. Nierenberg, *The Complete Negotiator* audio (New York: Simon & Schuster Sound Ideas, 1989).
(Nierenberg was nicknamed "The Father of Negotiating" by the Wall Street Journal.)

"[Negotiating is] an exchange of information and ideas with the purpose of reaching a decision that's mutually accepted by all parties involved." George F. Donohue, *Real Estate Dealmaking* page 41 (Chicago: Dearborn Trade Publishing, 2005).

"Negotiation is the process of overcoming obstacles in order to reach agreement." Ed Brodow *Negotiation Boot Camp: How to Resolve Conflict, Satisfy Customers, and Make Better Deals* page 9 (New York: Doubleday, 2006).

Mr. Brodow makes an excellent point when he explains that negotiating is about collaborating, not just about winning.

"Negotiation is the sum of all the ways in which we convey information about what we want, what we desire, and what we expect from other people—as well as how we receive information about other people's wants, desires and expectations." George Ross, *Trump Style Negotiation* page 5 (Hoboken: John Wiley & Sons, 2006).

"Negotiating is the commerce of information for ultimate gain." Ronald Shapiro and Mark Jankowski, *The Power of Nice* page 17 (Hoboken: John Wiley & Sons, 2001).

Harvard's Nine Steps For Preparation Adapted to Real Estate Sales

1. Do the research to figure out what a good result would be from your client's point of view, and also what a good outcome would be for your counterpart. This practice gives you something to aim for, and you get a feeling for what the counterpart is aiming at. Using this information, you should anticipate the questions and objections that you will get, so you can rehearse your response.

2. Search for ways to create additional value in the sale, particularly from trading things of less value from one party to another party who values that item more. This procedure will give you ways to create more value in the transaction, and possibly claim more of the created value for your side.

3. Know your other choice, so that you know the value of your alternatives, and know your walk away price . Try to figure out what those items would be for your counterpart. By learning these items, you know when you will give up and have an idea when your counterpart will give up.

4. If your other choice is not particularly good, try to find ways to make it better. If you can make your other choices better, you will end up getting a better deal in this negotiation, or you will take the other choice. When the motivation level of the buyer and seller is similar, the person with the most choices has the most power.

5. Determine if the people you are negotiating with have the authority to make a deal. For real estate this usually means to make sure you have everyone who has to sign off on the transaction involved, so you avoid the surprise of having to sell the sale all over again to an essential party.

6. Educate yourself on who you are dealing with by finding out everything you can about the people, their style of negotiating, and how they are looking at the negotiations. If you know how they have framed the issue, how they think, and their personality type, you will be able to communicate better.

7. If you might have another transaction with your counterparts in the future, get some validation that your offer is fair and reasonable, which is usually done in real estate by using comparable values. Remember, other real estate agents are your repeat customers, so if you can present your offer as being reasonable, you will have a better relationship, and you will give your counterpart some material to convince their client that the offer is reasonable.

8. Be prepared for a bumpy ride, as the negotiations may not go as you originally planned, so figure out ways you can adjust and be flexible. Believe that surprises will happen and prepare your client to expect the unexpected. Then, when it happens, you will not over-react.

9. See how you can change the negotiating process in your favor. Try to structure the negotiations to make it more likely that they will succeed and create a game plan that will get you where you want to go.

Adapted from Harvard Business Essentials, *Negotiation*, (Boston: HBS Press, 2003).

Personality Types

There are many different authors who categorize personality into different types. While the main text uses Marston's DISC profiles, there are a number of other systems that may be useful to you.

If you want to get into a complicated system, the Enneagram will give you nine personality types, and help you deal with the others involved in your negotiations by giving you a detailed projection of what they are likely to do. While it is good at predicting behavior and telling you how to deal with a certain personality type, I find it is too complicated and requires a great deal of analysis to determine which of the nine categories the person belongs to. If you want to look into this system take a look at *The Enneagram Made Easy* by Renee Baron and Elizabeth Wagele.

There are other writers who describe particular types of negotiators that may be useful to you. In *The Only Negotiating Guide You'll Ever Need*, Peter Stark and Jane Flaherty categorize negotiators as Amiable (negotiators who need to feel recognized and valued in the process, while they focus on relationships), Drivers (results oriented, bottom line negotiators), Analytical (negotiators who explore every option in detail looking for a fair result) and a Blend (negotiators who use a combination of styles—that's me). They also have suggestions on how to build an effective relationship with each type of negotiator.

Similarly, in *The Strategy of the Dolphin*, Dudley Lynch and Paul Kordis categorize negotiators into Sharks (win-lose negotiators who want to get as much as they can, regardless of the collateral damage), Carps (negotiators who work in a framework of scarcity, then try not to lose) and Dolphins (negotiators who can adapt and use multiple strategies).

The Weekend Millionaire Secrets to Negotiating Real Estate by Mike Summey and Roger Dawson, presents another way to categorize people, using two main factors, assertiveness and emotion, to develop four groups of people, which range from unassertive non-emotional people to highly assertive highly emotional people. They label their groups Pragmatic (high assertive, low emotion), Extroverts (high assertive, high emotion), Amiables (low assertive, high emotion) and Analyticals (low emotion, low assertive). They believe that these eight categories will give you a way to deal better with your counterparts, as you will try to adapt your negotiating to their personality type.

Eventually, you will develop your own system to understand yourself and the others involved, and to predict the behavior of your counterparts.

Acknowledgements

Thanks to my daughter Laurie Burrell Hughes who kept insisting that I write down what I know about real estate negotiating, and for making great improvements in my first draft of the book. Thanks to my son, Jeff Burrell, for teaching me how poker mimics much of negotiating, then out negotiating me at the poker table.

The Allen F. Hainge CyberStars™, and Allen Hainge himself, have been instrumental in creating this book. Margaret Rome was a great teacher as she shared what she learned in writing her book, provided ideas for the first draft, and encouraged me every step of the way. Thanks to Chris Laurence, Barbara Gaines and Ron Street for reading the book's first draft and making suggestions that improved the quality of the finished product. Thanks to all the other CyberStars™ who gave me negotiating stories and taped video interviews for **www.CreateAGreatDeal. com.**

Thanks to Bill Owens of RE/MAX UNITED not only for reading the book's first draft and suggesting improvements, but for allowing me to teach negotiating for RE/MAX UNITED so I could practice getting my ideas into Realtor's heads. Thanks to Sandra Sanders of RE/MAX Palos Verdes for allowing me to teach at her firm and encouraging me to write this book.

I appreciate the extra effort by my team of real estate agents, the Team For YOUr Dreams: Lisabeth Tunell, Anthony Williams, Bob Rodwell, Marilyn Irish, Maureen Fortin and Judy Burrell. They all worked extra hard so that I could concentrate on this book.

The advice of Rob Levy, Galand Haas and Joe Lininger of RealPro Systems has been extremely valuable. Thanks for all the meetings and discussions.

My publisher, Peg Silloway, has been the perfect guide, explaining the difference for each decision in the publishing process and providing top quality advice. Kathleen Silloway did a wonderful job editing the text and convincing me to make some changes I would not have made without her guidance.

I learned much of my negotiating from Ken and Lorna Burrell, my parents, because I grew up in the real estate business. Watching them negotiate at the earliest stages of my life gave me the background to learn this art. Bruce Burrell, my brother, gave me some of the best phrases in this book while we discussed it over a glass of wine.

My deepest gratitude is to my wife, Judy, who not only put up with all the time it took to write and rewrite this book, but she took over much of the work at my real estate office to free up my time. She was a great help with editing and is the Princess of Photoshop, as she created the graphics for the cover and the first page of each chapter. I married extremely well.

My special thanks goes to all of my clients who gave me the opportunity to practice the art of real estate negotiating.

THE REAL ESTATE NEGOTIATING INSTITUTE

There are some real estate skills that you can learn quickly, like entering listings in the MLS, taking pictures for virtual tours or working a lockbox. They are simple skills that take little judgment or finesse. There are other talents that are more like ballet...reading one book, going to one seminar or taking one lesson will not do it. You need to study negotiating, then practice it, try it, analyze the experience, fine tune it, try it the next time, then reflect on it. You have to gradually develop the skills to be able to fully practice the art of negotiating. The Real Estate Negotiating Institute gives everything you need to fully develop negotiating talent.

The Institute has the advantage of providing an education that is focused on real life real estate, not just theories of how to negotiate in a business meeting. You could read all the Harvard Treatises and Pro Sports negotiating books, then try to adapt the principles to your daily life in real estate. Instead, the Institute does it for you.

The Institute provides the latest education online, where you can read material focused on real estate that is regularly updated. Also, the Institute gives you the ability to participate in nationwide discussions of negotiating issues so that you can learn from the experiences of top agents from all over the United States. Check out the ideas posted in the member's only section, then participate by putting in your own thoughts so that you can develop and fine tune your judgment. You can also participate in Webinars to continue your education and practice.

What will this do for you?

- You will put together more deals, from listings, to sales, to referrals, to repair solutions, to post closing solutions. In other words, you will have more sales from the same number of leads.
- You will put deals together more smoothly, with less aggravation.
- You will keep more deals together and have them close more easily.
- You will have more satisfied customers, as they get their goals accomplished, frequently by giving less and getting more.
- You will have better relationships with other Realtors, as they will appreciate working with someone who can make a sale work and make it work gracefully.
- You will have a better, less stressful life because your relationships with your clients and your peers will be improved.
- You will contribute to the professional image of real estate agents.

If you are interested in more information on the Real Estate Negotiating Institute, go to **www.CreateAGreatDeal. com** and click on the **Negotiating Institute** tab.

About the Author

Tim Burrell grew up on the Palos Verdes Peninsula, near Los Angeles, California as a member of a family of home builders and Realtors, so his exposure to real estate negotiating started early. He graduated from Pomona College in Claremont, California, and negotiated admission to UCLA Law School (using a competing offer of a full scholarship to USC Law School). He has been a California Attorney since 1973, starting his career in real estate litigation and negotiating over real estate development permits.

Tim Burrell has been a real estate broker since 1979. The unusual thing about his career is its wide range. He sold luxury real estate on the Palos Verdes Peninsula in California for 16 years with Burrell Realty, his own firm. In 1996, he relocated to Raleigh, NC where he currently lives. He led a team of Realtors in Palos Verdes, California with RE/MAX Palos Verdes while at the same time he led a team of Realtors with Prudential Carolinas Realty and RE/MAX UNITED in Raleigh, NC. He has sold multi-million dollar luxury homes on one end of the spectrum and under $25,000 bank owned properties (REOs) on the other end.

On the one hand, Tim has run his own firm, and on the other he has been an agent for Prudential and RE/MAX. On one extreme, he represents first time homebuyers and on the other represents investors with many, many properties. He does "short sales" for his clients as well as agents around the United States, where he "grinds" the banks. Then on the opposite side he represents banks selling REOs. He is a member of www.REObroker.com, representing bank owned properties on one end of the client spectrum and on the other end he has been a member of the Institute of Luxury Home Marketing, representing "Rich Buyers and Rich Sellers." He is a top agent with technology, as a member of the CyberStars™, but he prefers to talk to people face to face. As a part of his family construction company, he created subdivisions and homes in California. In contrast, he started his professional career as an environmental attorney representing citizen's groups opposed to developments. The range of experience has given him a practical education in nearly all parts of real estate negotiations.

Tim is a member of RE/MAX Hall of Fame and he has received the Legend Award in Prudential Real Estate. He has stacks of plaques. Tim is a member of the National Association of REALTORS®, and a member of its Council of Residential Specialists with the CRS designation. Of course, he has the Certified Negotiation Expert (CNE) designation. He has been a speaker at national conventions for Prudential, taught classes in negotiating for Prudential and RE/MAX and helped hundreds of agents who call or line up at his door.

In this book, Tim has pulled together his life of negotiating experience with a mission to teach this art to real estate agents and establish continuing learning with the Real Estate Negotiating Institute.

Index

CPSIA information can be obtained at www.ICGtesting.com
Printed in the USA
236306LV00003B/111/P